# DUDS

## HOW THE OIL CAME NORTH

*To Alex*
*"I was there"*
*McInnes*
*All the best*

*[signature]*

*XMAS 2009*

# John C Milne

PlashMill Press

Published in Scotland and the United Kingdom in 2009 by PlashMill Press

First Edition

Cover Photograph Courtesy *The Press and Journal*
Typography and Cover Design Copyright© 2009 PlashMill Press

A CIP catalogue record for this book is available from the British Library.

ISBN-13: 978-0-9554535-8-8

Printed by Robertson Printers, Forfar

PlashMill Press
The Plash Mill
Friockheim
Angus DD11 4SH
Scotland.

www.plashmillpress.com

# Contents

## *Dedication*

In Loving Memory of my Mother Daphne Jean Leslie Forbes, who used to caikle at my letters home (especially the couthy bits) and encouraged me to write more.

I'm sorry I'm late, Ma.

# Preface

A good deal has been written and recorded on the benefits of the successful exploitation of the North Sea Oil Bonanza. Most of the written work covers the technical advances in offshore drilling, platform construction and oil production technology and relates chiefly to the "Boom" years following the Oil Crises of 1973 and 1979. Quite a bit has been said on the economic effects, again mostly covering the hydrocarbon production years from 1975 onwards. Unfortunately, even more newsprint and film footage has been dedicated to the disasters and failures along the way of this great adventure and we must never forget them. Not much attention has been given to the early years of North Sea development and even less to the coverage of activities in the onshore sector.

According to the old adage about the nail, the horseshoe, the steed, the soldier, the army, the battle and the war, every link in a chain is of equal importance to ensure success in any project or campaign. Based on four decades of exposure to the industry and my experiences of the changes within it is my contention is that the links the North Sea supply chain, as represented by the activities in onshore logistics support, are of equal importance to the offshore heroics, but have generally been discounted or overlooked altogether. Future students of the history of the period could be excused for thinking that not much happened during the years of 1965-1975 and that all the most significant events occurred in the cold grey sea far from the sight of land. This is my humble attempt to help redress the balance.

As a proud Aberdonian I have wallowed in the delight that the fantastically successful international oil and gas business eventually arrived on our doorstep and have celebrated the fact that my family, friends and many associates have shared in the considerable economic and cultural success accompanying the juggernaut. Nowadays I am on first name terms with several millionnaires, which is something I could never have contemplated in 1969; however, in witnessing all that has happened since then, I am disappointed that there are no billionaires in my wide circle of friends, and that is not intended as a joke. The opportunities existed but, as I hope to explain as I go along, there are a few features of our communal psyche that guide us toward missing out on the main chance and settling within our comfort zone.

"History is written by the winning side." I think it was Churchill who first made that comment, although others probably have made similar observations. Those who have reaped the greatest benefits in terms of financial rewards and prestigious honours are not always those who have made the most significant efforts and contributions. Life is not fair and we cannot change that. As we watch and listen in despair as the least deserving claim all the credit for the good things that fall into their path by the creativity and labours of others we are conditioned to exercise forbearance and hope the unsung heroes will receive their rewards in heaven. With beatitudes you can expect platitudes. Poppycock.

I believe that the individuals and teams who make the difference deserve the praise and I hope to give an airing to the stories of some unsung heroes who should have earned respect from a wider audience. At the same time I will do my best to deflate some hot-air balloons but it is a sad fact that successful people are persuaded to believe their own publicity and theirs are the books that fly off the shelves.

Another favourite maxim, originally ascribed to Confucius, is that in order to see into the future we must have a good understanding of the past. We are approaching the end of the extremely profitable years of oil and gas production from the North Sea but that need not mean the end of opportunity or the cessation of meaningful employment. On the contrary we are now passing through the gates of a new path to progress and now is the best time to consider the gains we have made along with our mistakes and try to ensure we establish our region's position as a leading provider of people, goods and services for the still vibrant international energy business.

One of my favourite reads is the autobiographical memoir of the old Hollywood star David Niven. In this most entertaining publication Niven says that there are only two types of book. In the minority are those written to entertain the reader. The majority are written for the entertainment of the writer. As this is my first publication I hope this book stays in the minority.

This is not an autobiography. It is a memoir of my observations and represents my personal view of some of the events that I witnessed in the early days of onshore support for the fledgling North Sea exploration project and I hope that I can convey the significance of the efforts and contribution of the key players without focusing too much on my own involvement.

As it is a personal account and not an attempt at a history book, this has excused me from doing extensive research and I have avoided the painstaking trawl through dusty archives and weighty reference tomes. I have, however, checked my commentary with some of those key individuals in the various episodes and have been assured by them that my recollections are sufficiently accurate to merit their support and I would like to thank them for their honesty and continuing friendship. They know who they are but, as befits the innate modesty of the people of our region, they have asked not to be named.

Although the tale is intended to follow a chronological path from the Spring of 1969 to the end of 1973 and most of the names, places and dates should stand scrutiny, I have used a certain amount of literary licence in combining some disparate events to help convey something of the general tone of the era and the characters involved. Above all I have tried to keep the story entertaining. We should not let adherence to the facts interfere with a good story. As well as learning a lot during this period I had a lot of fun.

I also have had a load of fun in writing these pieces and hope you enjoy reading them.

# 1. Dubs – Past and Future

"Dubs" is a term, used in Aberdeen and the Northeast of Scotland, to describe all types of mud, ranging from "plitery dubs," the thin, slithery sort that is found in rain puddles and dirties your wellies, to "sharny dubs," that mix of soil and animal waste that sticks to everything and anything in the farmyard and is the single factor that probably hastened the invention of power washers.

In the Spring break from University in 1969 I was at a loose end. Jobs were hard to find, money was tight and I was wondering where my next pint would come from. As I sauntered into the Students' Union Beer Bar in Upperkirkgate, I bumped into Alex Forbes, a second cousin of mine and someone I reckoned would have good contacts.

"Fit like, Alex, ony jobs?"

Alex was usually pretty well connected and a sociable type, always scouting out new projects and opportunities. We had worked together previously at Gordon Graham, an old family outfit which ran a drinks distribution business with a beer bottling plant down in the Aberdeen Harbour area. Alex's half brother Jim Simpson was their Assistant Manager and would usually be amenable to hiring all sorts of help for the menial, sloppy jobs in the Regent Road plant. I'd had a few earlier stints at bottle washing, crate stacking and van deliveries, during the holidays from Aberdeen Grammar School, and had thoroughly enjoyed the varied experiences, the physical exertion and the exposure to working life. Much as I had enjoyed those aspects, however, the rates of pay were dreadful. Three shillings and threepence per hour with time and a quarter for overtime—but you would always have eager schoolboys queuing up to take it.

"Jim's opened a new business doon in the Regent Road warehouse," Alex started. "Gordon Graham have stopped the bottling and sellt a the plant. Jim's set up on his ain and rented the warehouses for storing some kinda stuff for that new oil rig that's working aff shore."

"Fit kinda stuff?" I queried.

"Dubs," said Alex.

"Dubs?" I responded. "Plitery or sharny?"

"Well it's actually caa'd Drilling Mud, some kinda poodery stuff they mix up and send oot tae the oil rig on supply boats an pit it in the well tae drill, apparently."

Neither of us were particularly practical sorts nor given to technical matters. We had been brought up in the age of meritocracy to understand that the way to success and riches lay in brainwork. Self-improvement would come from intellectual pursuits rather than physical effort, which is why we were at University, after all, wasn't it?

"Onywey, Jim's looking for a couple of casual labourers tae handle a load o dubs arriving at his warehouse later this week. D'ye fancy it?"

"Fit's the pey like?"

"Six Bob an oor. Wi time and a half for overtime, but it's jist for a wik."

Setting aside all intellectual aspirations, we proceeded down to the Docks to check out our old haunt at Regent Road and see for ourselves what might be involved in this "Dubs" handling operation. We were to report to the gaffer Jimmy Gallan and make the arrangements. We both knew Jimmy Gallan, though not very well at that time. In the collection of drivers and storemen at Gordon Graham he stood out as the most capable, a dab hand at stowing crates, tying ropes and manoeuvring the lorry into the most inaccessible locations. He had a famous sense of humour and seemed to have a witticism for every event.

On beer deliveries the drivers always loaded full crates at the front and stowed the empty returns at the rear of the lorry. Because of their weight and uniformity the full crates usually held firm with only a light rope over the top. The empties were much more unpredictable and there were regular incidents when whole loads would be thrown off the back after a sharp corner or sudden stop, which is the reason that every lorry carried a brush and shovel. Jimmy held a proud record of never having dropped a load. On one of the rare occasions when I had been his "lorry loon" on a circuit of the dockside bars, as we pulled away from The Market Arms en route to "Flannie's Bar" (a distance of only 100 yards,) I remarked to Jimmy that we had not secured the empties.

Deadpan he replied, "It's aa right, they canna faa, there's naethin haudin 'em!"

With a flash of a smile he started the motor, slipped it into gear and rolled cautiously downhill to Flannie's without a jolt, his cargo safe and ten minutes saved by not having to mess with the ropes.

When we reached Regent Road we found the old warehouse, but without its familiar trademarks. Instead of the Gordon Graham sign there was a hastily assembled board announcing "Aberdeen Service Company, Tel 56349." In the cobbled lane the old Ford Thames flatbed lorry had been repainted in a dusty blue with the new company name handwritten on the fuel tank. All the bottling plant had disappeared and it was quite amazing how much space had been created. In the old returns bay, where we had sorted millions of empty bottles and crates a new tenant, Schlumberger, had installed all manner of sophisticated electronic gadgetry. Next to that, where the antiquated bottle washer had stood, there was an empty hall where BP had assumed occupancy (sharing with Amoco, which was a harbinger of a future association) and in the store we had used for maturing bottles of Bass and Guinness (10-14 days otherwise they were undrinkable, although daily "samples" had been allowed for) there were stacks of wooden pallets with sacks of chemicals in a variety of foreign labels, such as Baroid, Hoechst, and Monsanto.

Going through what had been the secure store, where the full crates of beer were once stacked, there was now a small office with a row of different coloured telephones and more piles of exotic sounding chemicals. It was here we met Jimmy Gallan wearing his trademark black beret and dust covered dungarees.

3

"Fit are you idle buggers up till?" Not an unfamiliar greeting.

"We're here to see about a 'casual'—lifting dubs," said Alex, reminding Jimmy that he was Jim Simpson's brother. "Jim said to come and see you about starting."

"But you twa are students. A yer brains is in yer heid. I tellt Simpson I needed hardy loons tae help us wi this ruck o brighties. Ah'm nae sure you eens can handle it."

Jimmy mentioned "brighties," which we subsequently understood to be barytes, a finely powdered form of Barium Sulphate, an extremely heavy compound, insoluble in water and used as a weighting material in the composition of drilling mud (dubs.)

"Ach, well," Jimmy continued, "There's naebody else, so ye'll jist hiv tae dae. Come on through tae the coal hole an hae a shottie."

The "coal hole" was the front part of the warehouse complex, which had been used up until recently by Aberdeen Coal Company for storing and bagging bulk coal. Not for the first or last time coal was being replaced by oil. As we proceeded gingerly over the uneven cobbles bestrewn with black dross we could see that it was now almost half full of sacks of cement and other materials. Jimmy led us to the lowest pile of barytes and, with a half smile, invited us to pick up a sack.

From previous experience he knew that we could handle beer crates. A full beer crate weighs between 30-40 pounds and with built in grab handles is relatively easy to lift and stow. A sack of barytes comprised 50 Kilogrammes (110 pounds) of powder tightly packed in a multi-layered paper sack stitched on the ends. A reasonable design for storage but problematical for lifting and handling.

As we huffed and hawed, making lame excuses about being out of training, wearing the wrong gear etc, Jimmy asked us to stand back and watch how an expert did it. In 1969 Alex and I were probably as close as we would ever get to our physical prime. Alex was a stocky five foot nine and had been in the running for selection as a prop-forward for Junior Scotland Rugby XV. My frame had stretched to nearly six foot and, through football and beer, had begun to fill out to man-size proportions.

Although we were both clad fashionably but inappropriately in flares and seersucker shirts, we should have been able to manipulate these innocuous items with ease, but the leaden lump resolutely resisted our initial efforts to budge it, never mind lift it. Jimmy was in his early thirties, a slender five foot seven, about ten stone, soaking wet, but he fairly showed us.

"The secret is to roll the corners till ye get a haud then rug it an humph it an Bob's yer uncle, or raither, Simpson's yer uncle, which is how ye're here. "

In a flash he had the hundredweight sack off the cobbles, onto his knee and up on to his shoulder before plopping it back it on to the top of the pile.

"An at's anither thing ye'll need tae mind. Fan yer lifting this stuff, ye only want tae lift it once—nae double handlin."

We were both too inexperienced to understand the physical and commercial aspects of ergonomics and isometrics but we had learned right there and then and went on to discover over the years that Jimmy Gallan, with little formal education but a lot of experience, from a mainly agricultural background from Friockheim to Fyvie, had a Ph.D. in common sense and could apply his wits to any mechanical handling problem.

"Richt, ye'll start the morn at eight o'clock. Pit on yer aul' claes an bring yer ain piece. There's nine hunner ton o' barytes comin in an you twa will hiv tae muck in. Can ony o ye drive..."

"I've a licence." Alex interjected, proudly.

"...a fork-lift?" Jimmy concluded.

We both shook our heads. I had tried to learn to drive in my father's 1957 Hillman Minx but had yielded to the conclusion that I had insufficient mechanical aptitude. Alex had passed his driving test recently and, though eager to show his prowess in his mother's Renault Dauphine, was wary at the prospect of handling forklifts, which at that time were fairly rare. We looked at the imposing beast of yellow painted metal with the protruding forks, high mounted seat and a bold "Coventry Climax" emblazoned on the tall mast.

5

"Aw right, you twa'll dae the humphin an Jock an me'll dae the drivin."

Jock Smith appeared from the depths of the coal hole. A blustering bear of a man, Alex had recognised him and, in an aside, told me that Jock was the fearsome "Bouncer" at the Kingsway Bingo, who had acted as bodyguard for "Swifty" Rennie, a notable local bookie with many friends but also a few resentful clients seeking recompense for perceived injustices. Jock, reputedly, could handle himself.

"D'ye wint this pile o' shite shiftin, Jimmy?"

Both Jimmy and Jock gave a sideways glance at Alex and myself then, thankfully, a more considered stare at a pile of old barytes sacks and bits of broken pallets lying in the corner of the Coal Hole.

"Aye," said Jimmy "We'll need tae tak thon new pallets inside an get them ready for the nine hunner ton o barytes comin in the morn. If we leave them oot they'll be ta'en. Ye cannae trust naebody roon hereaboots. Damn Toon Dirt!"

As fork-lift trucks were rare, so too were pallets and, with a limited supply, a shortage of timber and a thriving "black" economy, anything that was not locked up would soon "walk." Jock was no economist but was well acquainted with most sources and outlets for scarce commodities and, as we would learn over the years, could turn a shilling out of the least likely items. He clambered on to the Coventry Climax, started it up, grabbed at the levers, stamped on the pedals and started to manoeuvre it towards the pile of rubbish. Jimmy winced at the sound of crashing gears and hissing hydraulics and in a smiling admonition cried out.

"Aye, Jock, haud er gaun, ye'll find a gear in their somewyes. Min' oot for the reef fan ye're pickin up the forks." Then he turned to his new hired hands. "We'll see you twa the morn,. Eight o'clock, min' an' dinna be late."

We were told that a cargo vessel was due in Aberdeen to discharge a cargo of 900 tons of sacked barytes from Morocco. It was to be berthed early the next day on Blaikie's Quay, where dockers would unload from the hold and have the sacks discharged on to lorries at quayside for delivery around the corner (a distance of 200-300yards.) Jimmy Gallan had worked out that the best way to handle the cargo would be for the dockers to "break bulk" and stow the sacks on to the new pallets in the hold, then load by crane direct onto his lorries and offload by fork-lift at the coal hole. But he reckoned without the machinations of the National Dock Labour Board. There was a fair amount of labour unrest in 1969 and disputes arising from restrictive practices were common.

With Jimmy's upbringing and forward thinking philosophy, he would hold no truck with what he perceived as wasteful handling, and his response was predictable when the dockers opened the hatches and observed that the 900 tonnes of sacks had been loaded individually. They immediately called a meeting to discuss how to handle the discharge. The meeting was convened at 0815 and lasted a little over an hour, taking the dockers close to their "Smoko," which meant that nothing could start until after 1000. The outcome of the meeting was that, as the cargo had been stowed individually, the dockers decided it would need to be offloaded individually (requiring two squads of eleven men each,) into rope cargo baskets and discharged individually on to the back of lorries (Unionised Transport only—in support of their Brothers.) Jimmy was apopleptic. This meant that his trucks would be idle and his expensive pallets redundant.

"Dockers! Ah've shit better!"

I have never been any use at rising in the morning and it was not good timing to toddle in sleepy-eyed at 0900 just as Jimmy was getting the message about the Dockers' decision. I mumbled some sort of apology and offered to help out where I could.

"Students! Ye're near as bad as dockers, it's jist as weel ther's naethin here yet or youd've gotten seckit afore ye startit!" He put his hand in his pocket, took out a Half Crown. "Gaun tae the Café an' get fower bacon rolls afore the place gets swampit wi' thon lazy bastards."

I grasped the coin and ran off to the Oak Tree Tea Rooms, the quaintly named "Greasy Spoon" masquerading as a restaurant amid the open fish boxes, coal stew and barytes dust of Regent Road. Alex had made the tea by the time I returned to dole out the steaming baps and, as I gave Jimmy his twopence change, anticipating a further rocket, he surprised me with his calm appraisal of the situation.

"Right, if they're nae gaun tae load thae pallets we're jist gaun tae dae it oorsels. One o you can help the driver tae affload, the ither ane'll help Jock tae stow an I'll dae the forkie. Jock, tak the larry load o pallets back fae Blaikie's an pit them in the road ootside. You twa can lay them oot in a row alongside the pavement. The porters'll be awa' hame syne an we'll need a their car parkin space tae haud the pallets."

The "porters" that Jimmy referred to were Fish Market Porters, who started their shift very early in the morning and finished about nine or ten o'clock. Aberdeen was still a leading fishing port and with growing affluence, more of the porters had acquired motorcars and usually nabbed the increasingly valuable parking spaces in Regent Road.

Jock returned from Blaikie's Quay with the Thames laden with new wooden pallets, each carefully stencilled, on the end bars, "A.S.C." as a deterrent to any keen eyed "recycler." It was easy to tell from the variety of names on the thousands of fish boxes that lay all over the Aberdeen Harbour district that wooden containers of any type were cherished but not many of them had made it back to their original owners in Arbroath, Pittenweem, Mallaig, Lochinver and other distant fish markets.

A quick scan through the Regent Road warehouse revealed pallets with unfamiliar stencils of ICI, Wiggins Teape, GKN and others. Over the years Jock proved to be as effective a "recycler" of pallets as his fish market cronies had proven in the field of fish boxes. He was fiercely loyal, however, and it was seldom that anyone spotted a pallet emblazoned with the "A.S.C." logo anywhere but in its rightful place. Alex and I helped to lay out the pallets at Jimmy's direction as the first load of barytes arrived on the back of a green lorry.

"Damn the bit! They've gotten BRS tae dae the haulin'. BRS cairters–they're a' Toon Dirt worse 'n dockers. We'll hiv tae dae that an a'. Right, you twa up on tae the wagon and ca' them ower."

The inference was that BRS drivers were all Aberdeen (Toon) based and as members of the Transport & General Workers Union, would not be willing to help with offloading. Jimmy held a view that only "Country Loons" i.e. those from outside the City Limits, were fit for this kind of labour.

This is a prejudice that could not be countenanced in the modern era but, over the piece, it is a judgement that most independent observers would support. Alex and I took comfort that, in our new Gaffer's eyes, we had achieved a status superior to both dockers and lorry drivers and took to the task with some gusto. We tore into the individually stowed sacks and lowered them on to the shoulders of Jock and Jimmy who placed them carefully on to the pallets we had earlier laid out on the roadside. Within half an hour we had offloaded the twenty tons of sacked barytes on to ten pallets and before the second lorry arrived Jimmy had managed to shift five of those and stacked them neatly in their allotted slot of the warehouse.

The second lorry arrived and, thankfully, according to the Jimmy Gallan rule of fitness, the driver was a "country loon," working for a non-unionised firm and, therefore, quite willing and able to help us with offloading. This meant that Alex was "promoted" to ground work, helping Jock with palletising while Jimmy concentrated on fork lift duties. As we watched the second lorry pull in to Regent Road, Jimmy handed me a blue note book and pencil.

"Can ye coont?" he inquired, hopefully.

"I'm a mathematical genius," I replied with cockiness born of the recent success from offloading twenty tons of barytes.

"Right, gaun coont that lot in the coal hole and write it doon in thon book."

"Four hundred," I retorted without a movement.

"How d'ye ken?" Jimmy looked quizzically.

"Easy," I said confidently, as mental arithmetic had always come naturally to me. "Ten pallets, forty sacks each, four hunner."

"Richt enough." Jimmy confirmed checking his handwritten notes in the blue book. " A' richt, you can keep coont fae noo on. Mind and write it a' doon."

Jimmy could count well enough but had never been as comfortable with paperwork as he was with "real work." Jock, pointedly, refused to have anything to do with reading and writing. Alex could count but his handwriting was dreadful so I had stumbled into an opportunity. I stuffed the notebook into my back pocket and jumped up on to the newly arrived lorry.

We made good progress with shifting the second lot. The driver was hardy and cheery and I struggled to keep pace with him. Jock and Alex were following Jimmy's instructions about overlapping the sacks and keeping the corners neat. This helped the stacking of the pallets Jimmy had whisked off into the coal hole with consummate skill.

By the time the second lorry had been offloaded he had the lot stowed and stacked in neatly palletised piles but as we approached twelve o'clock we knew that the dockers would be knocking off for lunch and no more loads would arrive. We too had a break but noticed that Jimmy never stopped. He tidied up the pallets and laid new ones out in preparation for the afternoon session. He asked for a running tally.

"Foo mony's that then, Brains?"

"Eight hunner," I responded, proud of my new position and title.

"Foo mony tae come?" It took me a few seconds to work it out.

"Seventeen thoosan' and twa hunner mair."

"We'll never get on at this rate."

He cursed and took off to the office while Alex and I made our way to the Oak Tree. Not for the first time and certainly not for the last, Jimmy worked through his lunch hour. In this instance he took the opportunity to collar Mike Kroeckl, who was the local manager of IMC (International Minerals Corporation.) They were the importers of the cargo of barytes and would be picking up the bill for all the handling costs. Aberdeen Service Company acted as

10

warehousing agents and had responsibility for receipt and despatch of all IMC's products. Jimmy took his responsibilities very seriously and was equally concerned about incurring extra costs for his clients as well as his employer.

When we returned from our mince and tatties Jimmy explained that there was a further change of plan. During the lunch break he had persuaded Mike Kroeckl to call his boss, Dick Cotton, in their Great Yarmouth office and inform him of the reasons for the slow progress. Although I did not know, at that time, all the vagaries of Ship Chartering and related charges involving Ship's Dues, Light Dues, Demurrage and the rest, I grasped, from Jimmy's urgency and Mike's anxiety, that something needed to be done to ensure that the 900 tons was transferred from the vessel to the warehouse in a maximum of four days and that, at the rate we were going, this might take up to two weeks, which nobody could afford. Jock Smith paraphrased the situation well.

"The Dockers'll be haudin' oot for "Dirty Money" or a bonus," he surmised.

"Aye, right, but they'd nae get naethin fae me." Jimmy assured everyone. "But Kroeckl's gotten Cotton tae stump up extra tae get them movin'."

In later years I would learn more of the tactics and strategies in motivating dockers, shipowners, Customs agents and all related in the cargo handling business but, for the time being, I left it to those who cared about it to sort it out. At that time I really cared mainly about my Six Bob an Hour but also had an inbred ethic for getting the job done with the minimum of fuss.

Jimmy went on to explain that the dockers would now be prepared to stow the cargo on to pallets in the hold of the vessel and crane them on to lorries (Unionised only so still no use for the ASC trucks). We would then offload by forklift and stack them in our warehouse. This would require a second forklift. Jimmy had already worked that out and had arranged for a rental truck to be sent from Barlow Handling. This was due to arrive at 2 o'clock, by which time the flow of loaded wagons would be putting a strain

11

even on the capabilities of Jimmy and his Coventry Climax.

As expected, with the "extra" payment, the flow of sacks was much improved and by the time the second forklift was delivered there were three BRS lorries queuing up outside Regent Road. Alex and I both realised that, with palletising already done, there might be no need for our services; however, when we mentioned this to our Gaffer, he responded in typical fashion.

"Ye canna trust dockers tae dae a richt job. Thon pallets'll be in a gey state by the time they get here and you'll need to square them up afore me an Jock stacks em. An we'll need "Brains" tae count faister if they keep comin at this rate."

The forklift that arrived from Barlow was very different from the Climax. This was a Henly Hawk with automatic transmission, power steering and much easier, gentler controls. Jimmy, naturally, adapted fairly quickly to the different handling characteristics but Jock struggled to cope with the changes. During a lull in the activity while the dockers and drivers had a further break, Jimmy explained the rudiments of the Henly to Alex and gave him a chance to handle a few pallets, which he achieved with surprising aplomb. His attempts with the Climax were less successful, however, but also noticeably more proficient than Jock's efforts. For the rest of that day and on through the week the three of them rotated on forklift duties while I toiled as pallet adjuster and clerk.

By the end of the first day, Tuesday, we had handled 120 tons=60 pallets=2400 sacks. Wednesday showed improved productivity and we took in 300 tons=150 pallets=6000 sacks. Thursday saw the same leaving a balance of 180 tons to arrive on the Friday to complete the discharge. Again Jimmy was prescient in his droll way.

"We can expect a rush this mornin'. Thae dockers winna want tae hing aboot on a Friday. As sure as a cat's a hairy beast they'll want tae get feenished, dustit doon an' intae the Harbour Bar as soon as their pey's in their pockets."

Just as Jimmy predicted the final 180 tons arrived in a rush. There were 3604 sacks to be exact (and I had counted, dutifully, every single sack) as the cargo was slightly above the nominal 900 tons and in spite of the couple of hundred sacks lost due to handling damage we could report to Kroeckl and Cotton that we had a full load palletised and stacked and safely secure in the coalhole ready for distribution.On the stroke of Twelve Noon the dockers duly dusted themselves off, changed into their "civvies" marched to the Payroll Office at John Cook & Son in Marischal Street, picked up their wages along with a handsome bonus and headed for their favourite haunt–the Harbour Bar–where an expectant Dougie Argo would be sure to give them a welcoming smile.

Alex and I helped Jimmy and Jock to re-bag some of the residual barytes that the dockers had swept out of the hold. As luck would have it, Mike Kroeckl strode purposefully out of the IMC office to announce that they had a sale for 100 tons of barytes to go on a supply boat loading out of Pocra Quay the next week. This was good news for IMC and for Aberdeen Service Company, as this would be the first delivery to the "Staflo" rig being operated by Shell UK who had, up until this point, been using the rival brand, British CECA. Our competitors, Barrack, did CECA's warehousing and transport. This was a chance to impress. The Gaffer's keen logistical mind clicked into gear.

"Jock, gaun fetch the bulker."

The "bulker" was an old, decrepit cement tanker from the building trade, still displaying the faded "Fyfestone" logo on the side, which had been sitting inside the coal hole looking fairly forlorn. Jock hustled over and with his usual display of fury and frustration managed to kick it into life and steer it towards the front door. Jimmy summoned Alex and me to help him manoeuvre another odd piece of machinery. This assembly of bars, belts and tubes was described as a "Papper-Up," a Lister Elevator, commonly used on farms for building haystacks ("Biggin' Rucks" in Jimmy's parlance.)

"Whoa! That'll dae, Jock," he shouted as we helped him guide the elevator alongside the bulker. "Right, you eens, haul thon 'sweepin's' ower tae the end o the papper-up."

Alex jumped on the Henly as Jimmy went to start up the diesel engine on the elevator. I straightened up the assortment of polythene and paper bags full of swept up barytes.

"Na, na," Jimmy said. "Nae the Hawk, that's gaun aff hire as seen as the Barlow mannie comes tae collect it. Tak' the 'beast'(the Climax.) Ye'll need tae learn foo tae handle that fae now on."

"Kroeckl, gaun tell us foo much barytes we can load tae thon bulker."

Mike Kroeckl was a fairly genial Rhodesian Mud Engineer and did not mind Jimmy's familiarity in the slightest. He was also pretty sharp at converting weights and volumes of powders and liquid, which is an essential for a Mudman. He used one of those new fangled hand held calculators and came back pretty sharpish.

"Going by the dimensions I reckon that you should get 27,500 pounds in there."

"Fit's that in real money?" Jimmy looked to me.

"That's aboot twelve and a half tons," I offered

"Hey, how do you know that?" Mike clicked his calculator and confirmed.

"I just worked it out in my head," I responded.

"An' foo mony bulker loads will we need to fill the twa fifty ton tanks at Pocra?" Jimmy challenged. "Come on Brains, work that ane oot."

"That'll be eight." I came back and Jimmy looked quizzically at Mike.

"Jimmy, you got yourself a clerk here, you don't need me and my gadget."

Mike returned to his office smiling, pleased with the prospect of a sale to a new customer and happy with the knowledge that the Aberdeen Service Company could tend to all the handling requirements. He later disclosed that the charges from the Ship's Agent including berthage, craneage, dockers and trucks had amounted to £3600 or £4 per ton. That was the first but not last mention I had heard which inferred that Aberdeen was an expensive place to do business. Aberdeen Service Company's fee (which I later found out was based on a percentage of all sales) for receiving, palletising, stacking, storage, breaking to bulk, delivery to quayside and discharge to supply vessel amounted to less than £2 per ton. No wonder he was smiling.

We filled the bulker by the very crude and simple method of loading the variety of sacks on to the elevator, cutting them with a knife and emptying them into the hatch at the top of the bulker. A modern day HSE inspector would tear his hair out at the methods but practicality and profitability were the priorities at that time. Jock took the bulker on to Pocra Quay and discharged the first load into the two-tone green IMC silo. Job done.

The Gaffer asked for the return of the blue notebook he had entrusted to me on the Tuesday and on opening it noticed no new markings of any sort.

"Hemmin, ye hinnae written onything doon!"

"That's right," I said. "I did it a' in ma heid."

Jimmy merely shrugged and took a ragged piece of paper out of the top of his dungarees.

"Jist as weel I was checking."

He pored over his carefully written tally of pallets and sacks and, after a few minutes, verified my mental calculations that we had received 18004 complete sacks and a bulker load of "sweepins". A grand total of 912 tons. Without saying anything more he then went on to complete the timesheets for the week before phoning the figures through to Maggie, Jim Simpson's wife, who did all the accounting and payroll.

Alex and I took our lunch break and by the time we had eaten Jock had returned from the quay, having successfully despatched the first batch of barytes. Maggie had also arrived with her usual cheery smile, bearing and dispensing the valued payslips.

"Aye, aye, Jimmy, ye've earned yer money this week."

"They're ye go, Jock. Dinnae gi'e it aa tae the bookie."

"Alex, mercy, ye'll need tae buy new breeks, that anes are a torn."

"There ye go, young John, mind an buy a sweetie for yer ma."

Jimmy merely stuffed his unchecked packet in his pocket and

carried on planning the next set of tasks. Jock took his and hurried off somewhere "urgent." Jock always had some urgent business somewhere. Alex opened his and joked.

"Maggie, far's ma bonus? Nae dirty money?"

"Ye're dirty enough already. Fit mair di' ye want?"

On opening my neatly inscribed manilla package I noticed that I had been paid, for four full days, eight hours a day, thirty-two hours at six shillings, nine pounds twelve shillings.

"Here, ye've overpaid me. Mind, I was late in an' missed an 'oor on Tuesday."

"Ach." Said Jimmy. "It's jist as weel I canna coont!"

With his usual good humour Jimmy would overlook minor indiscretions as long as he could see that a man was trying his best. He then went on to tell us that he had ordered some new pieces of equipment that would make for easier and safer bulk cutting and handling. He had designed and built a new cutting table with steel legs and an angled platform with a built-in paper cutting device. This could be operated at ground level so that we would not have to use the precarious table above the hatch of the bulker. He had also ordered an "Agger" which was an electric powered sort of Archimedes Screw (Auger) designed to convey the cut barytes from the new cutting table directly into the bulker. These new pieces of kit would eliminate the danger of falling, reduce the risk of damage to fingers and minimise the airborne dust, as well as speeding up the cutting process.

"I'll get the new machines riggit up o'er the weekend an' we'll get intae the bulkin' first thing Monday. Will you eens be fit tae come back for that?"

I had quite enjoyed the new experience and, although it had been very hard physical effort, I was intrigued to find out what this new machinery might offer; anyway I desperately needed the money so I agreed straight away. I'm not sure whether Alex shared my eagerness, as he mentioned having a lot of work to do for the Student's Charities Campaign, of which he was the Publicity Secretary, but he did volunteer the services of one of his Rugby playing mates and promised to send him along.

"Anither damn student? Ah, well, we'll jist hiv tae mak the best o't. There's nae point in daein ony mair the day. You eens'll be needin tae getting' awa an get riggit for yer Friday nicht oot."

At that we set off for the Students Union Beer Bar, money in pocket and a healthy thirst. The Regent Bridge had been swung closed for the weekend so we had to walk through the Fish Market, around the Albert Dock to Trinity Quay and up the Shiprow. We met some of the dockers hustling between Argo's and the bookies. Well loaded. There was some banter about how much they had been paid and how little we had been paid for our efforts. We felt we held the moral high ground if not the monetary benefit.

Approaching the Students Union we caught sight of ourselves in the dark glass windows and noticed that the faintly pink powdered barytes had lightened the colour of our dark curly hair and given our faces the effect of a decent suntan. As we headed for the Beer Bar our friendly barman Graham Paterson was rolling up the shutters. Before we could greet him or shout our order he observed our "bleached and tinted" appearance.

"Ay, ay, you twa been yer holidays?"

"Nah," Alex replied. "We've been workin' at the barytes. An' 'at's thirsty work. Gie's two pints o' lager."

"Barytes?" Graham queried, tilting the dimpled jugs into the "Harp" tap. "Fit's that?"

"Dubs!" we responded in unison.

"Dubs?" Graham looked at us quizzically, pouring and serving our pints.

"Aye, Dubs," said Alex "It's the future!"

# 2. "Augers ... Well?"

Just as the Telegraph did for the Pony Express and email would do for the Fax machine the Auger signalled the end for the "Papper Up" (Elevator.) With increasing demands for Drilling Mud (Dubs) during 1969 there were increasing pressures on the resources of Aberdeen Service Company to keep up the supply of bulk materials. Barytes, cement and bentonite were all packaged in paper sacks stored on wooden pallets at the Regent Road warehouse and "cut to bulk" into lorry mounted tankers for transport to the fifty ton capacity silos on Pocra Quay and Torry Dock. This was hard, dangerous and boring work, and finding men fit and able to do it was becoming more difficult.

Jimmy Gallan, the redoubtable "Gaffer" at "The" Service Company (as he, invariably described it, never its full title and only, reluctantly, later on as Asco, the moniker coined in 1972 by Alex Forbes and myself to reflect the internationalisation of the enterprise and to show affinity with our key customers like Amoco, Conoco, Arco, Texaco and Vetco,) was always at the centre of any practical innovation, and it was he who suggested the introduction of the Auger. This device was commonly used for carrying grain from trailers through hoppers into silos; Jimmy had used them on some of the more modern farms about the area and thought it would work better than the "Papper-Up." He also re-designed the cutting tables and hoppers to improve the handling of the heavy sacks and standardised the size of the wooden pallet to a five by four foot double sided layout, all of which contributed to increased productivity while greatly reducing any risk of damage to people or material. HSE? Jimmy was well ahead of his time in this respect.

Jim Simpson, too, was a visionary. The winter of 1969/70 was a busy one for the fledgling oil industry in Aberdeen, but since most of the activity was conducted 140 miles offshore the populace of the

19

city could be excused for not knowing about it. Jim Simpson was a natural entrepreneur but was struggling to manage the declining drinks distribution industry at Gordon Graham. Suffering amid the burgeoning influence of the powerful brewers, Scottish & Newcastle, United Caledonian and Usher Vaux Gordon Graham had passed its sell-by date. Jim also ran (or, rather, his charming wife, Maggie did) a Boarding House at 28, Balmoral Place which, in common with most other hostelries in those relatively depressed days, took a lot of effort to make a profit. They also owned a One Armed Bandit leasing company, Aberdeen Machines Ltd and, to eke out a living, Jim did occasional stints as Bingo Caller at the Kingsway.

By coincidence or Fate or whatever they had, as their guests at their boarding house, for a brief spell during 1964/65 two Geology students who had disclosed to Jim and Maggie, the most genial and hospitable entertainers, that their research work on the carboniferous strata in the Montrose Basin had been attracting a fair deal of interest from major oil companies such as BP and Amoco and that their extrapolations might indicate that there would be significant accumulations of oil and gas in the outer reaches of the northern part of the North Sea. Several gas fields had been discovered in the southern part and had engendered a "mini-boom" during the 1960's in Great Yarmouth, Lowestoft and other coastal ports. Further exploration off the north east of England using bases at Easington and Hartlepool had yielded little success and most accounts by informed commentators had dismissed the Northern Sector as distinctly unpromising. Jim Simpson was intrigued by the comments of his geologist lodgers and, from discussions with various other visitors from Gt. Yarmouth, London and places further afield he was encouraged to believe that the Northern Sector might evolve as something more than a passing fancy.

In his capacity as Assistant General Manager at Gordon Graham Jim had responsibility for the Bonded Warehouse (No.5 Bond) handling the Duty Free whisky from Long John and Black Bottle distilleries prior to general distribution. Bonded warehouses were strictly controlled and licensed by HM Customs & Excise and, therefore, a valuable asset. The Operators and major contractors in the North Sea had used the Bonded Warehouses in Great Yarmouth, Lowestoft and Hartlepool to import and store their valuable oilfield equipment and consumables on a Duty Suspended basis prior to despatch offshore. HM Customs Tariff rates ran pretty high at that time in the range of 5% to 33% and so represented a significant cost exposure in the already expensive venture of offshore drilling. It was no coincidence then that the early scouts seeking out premises and facilities for storage and handling would beat a path to Jim Simpson's door.

One of these early visitors was Dick Cotton of International Minerals & Chemicals (IMC) a division of Halliburton. He had made the call at the behest of Mitch Watt, an affable but pugnacious displaced Scot who was in charge of Amoco's exploration programme. Mitch had suggested that, if IMC wanted any part of their business in the Northern Sector, they had better get their "asses" up to Aberdeen and seek out mud handling facilities for their next round of drilling. On Dick's scouting trip he called at Customs House on Regent Quay and enquired which companies held the Bonded Warehouses. He was directed next door to Gordon Graham's where he first met Jim Simpson. After a preamble and a cup of coffee Dick Cotton outlined IMC's requirements for a Bonded Warehouse, storage facilities, forklifts, lorries, bulkers, offices, men and equipment, in summary, a "Service Company." Jim, ever the man with an eye for an opportunity, responded;

"Dick, you've come to the right place. We have just what you want. It's called "Aberdeen Service Company." It has all that you need, the whole shebang. "Have a dram." Jim reached for a Fifteen Year Old Laphraoig and pulled the stopper.

"Yeah?" queried Dick, accepting a fine Edinburgh Crystal glass. "Who owns it?"

"I do," said Jim, proudly, though he had not, as yet, any such Company nor any men, trucks or facilities. He started thinking very quickly how he could proceed without blowing this very impressive cover.

"That's great!" Dick smiled as Jim topped up his glass. "When can we go and see what you got? I'd like to take our Warehouse Manager with us."

"I've got a better idea," Jim interjected, "Why don't we come down and visit your place in Yarmouth, see how you do things down there and then we can fix things up here to suit your way of working?"

"Good thinking, Batman," quipped Dick. "How soon can you come down?"

"How about Monday week? I'll bring my Foreman down so he can eyeball your operation and let us know what we need to fix you up." Jim was already thinking who would be the best bet as his "Foreman."

"Sounds fine." They both supped their drams and agreed to meet a week later.

Over the weekend Jim informed Arthur Whyte, his boss at Gordon Graham, of the meeting with IMC and outlined his vision of the opportunities available. Whyte was of the "Old School" of business management; haughty, aloof, authoritarian and not very adaptable. Although he had no time for his underlings he could be fairly charming with customers, especially well-heeled ones, and with his perceived "superiors." He too was aware that their existing drinks distribution business was on the slide but, as he approached retirement, he was not as eager as Jim obviously was to exploit the North Sea potential. Agreeing to Jim's hurried proposal, Whyte sanctioned the sale of two flatbed lorries that had become surplus to requirements following the move of Gordon Graham from Market Street and Regent Road into single reduced premises on Regent Quay. More significantly he persuaded the owners of the family to transfer the lease on the Regent Road warehouse from Gordon Graham to the new outfit. In return for these efforts he became Jim Simpson's partner in the fledgling Aberdeen Service Company (albeit in their wives' names).

Jim had quickly worked out who his Foreman would be. In his time at Gordon Graham he must have seen a hundred drivers come and go, but one stood out as the prime candidate—Jimmy Gallan—and so he approached him with a view to a job change.

"Jimmy, how do you fancy working for me?"

"Fit are ye on aboot? I already work fer ye."

"Aye, but this'll be slightly different."

Jim explained the proposed change of plan, change of ownership, different working conditions, extra responsibilities and…an extra five pounds a week.

"Fan div I start?" Jimmy was always eager, but an increase from £12 to £17 a week was a significant incentive in 1967 to a "Fairmer's loon" with a young family.

"You start Monday. I want you to clean out the old Regent Road warehouse and dress up the old flatbed trucks. We'll have to get a fork-lift truck and some other kit, and I'll need you to come down with me on a visit to Great Yarmouth to check out how IMC do their handling and storage. How are you fixed for next Friday?"

"Nae bother, will I need a passport?" They both laughed.

I should mention to the reader at this point that, as I was not around any of these characters in 1967, I was not privy to any of the conversations, however, as I did get to know all of the main players quite well over time, the anecdotal evidence passed on to me over the years should bear scrutiny. I did not, officially, join "The" Service Company until June 1st 1970, before which time I had tried as hard as I could to get a job of any description anywhere else but back at Regent Road.

Over the winter of 69/70 I had devoted my time equally to football, snooker and carousing. Half my time was spent sleeping and generally recovering from these pursuits with the result that my studies, which should have been the main focus of attention, had suffered.

Hegelian Dialectics, Durkheim's Rules of Sociological Method, Robert K Merton's Theory of Anomie and others I cannot recall were all cast to the backburner where they remain to this day.

23

Without getting into too much of an intellectual dissertation I admit that I had woven myself into a sort of mental "loop" and I could not come to terms with the thought of grasping esoteric theories that could not be applied with any degree of certainty to real everyday problems. As I could not cope with that conundrum I could not finish my Thesis nor sit my Final Exams so I "dropped out." Although I still held out vague hopes of some day completing my MA (Honours) Sociology, I had to face the urgent need to find a job to pay my way.

For the first time in my life I put myself in the "Dole Queue" and ventured down to the bottom of Market Street to find myself at the "Broo" (Bureau of Employment) desk of Clerical Officer Stanley "Spike" Milligan. We recognised each other from school as he had been in the year above me at Aberdeen Grammar and, though there was usually little personal exchange between pupils of different forms, we were both fairly amiable coves and happy to acknowledge each other.

"Ony jobs, Spike?"

"Fit are you needin' a job for? Thought you were one o' the brainy ones."

Within about thirty seconds I summarised the past four or five years since we had last crossed each other's path. I think Spike got the message that I needed money and was genuinely keen to work for it rather than try to claim the "Dole." I did not need to explain the economic situation to Spike. Aberdeen was a bit more depressed than the rest of Britain in 1970 and there were lots of candidates for any vacant positions, not that there were many of those available.

On the day prior to my visit to the "Broo" I had indulged myself with aspirations of joining the Executive Gravy Train. Armed only with a handful of "Highers" and a bucket-load of blind ambition I had sauntered into the offices of Aberdeen Appointments Agency. In 1970 AAA was one of only two private organisations handling commercial and clerical openings. I filled in a form and was ushered into a private office where a pleasant, smiling middle-aged man welcomed me with a firm handshake and asked me to take a seat while he perused my particulars. After a few hums and haws he opened the conversation by asking the expected general enquiries about hopes, plans etcetera before throwing the "Curve Ball."

"What's your neck-size?"

"Sixteen and a half," I replied, nonplussed.

"Ideal, we have a position at Paton's in George Street. I know the proprietor very well and can get you an interview."

"Oh." I enthused, knowing nothing about Paton's but hoping they might have some kind of Junior Executive slot into which I could glide comfortably. "What sort of position?"

"Meat Porter," the avuncular AAA man responded without a murmur of irony. "With your height and build you'll be perfect. Let's call Mr Paton."

"No need," I blurted out. "I think I'll need some time to think about it."

Not a lot of time was required for further consideration. I think I remembered my manners and thanked the jovial gentleman before heading for the exit. I had the message loud and clear.

> There were no attractive jobs in Aberdeen.
> The few available jobs were menial and poorly paid.
> My "Qualifications" were worthless.

I could have done what I had done for the previous four years between University terms and headed for London where jobs were more plentiful and better paid but I was then (and still am) hopelessly in love with my gorgeous girlfriend (now my gorgeous wife) and she had one more year remaining to complete her studies at College of Education. She was staying in Aberdeen and I did not want to leave her so I thought hard for all of five minutes and resolved to take any job that was going. That was why I had made my way to Market Street. Some of my snootier former pupils might have gloated on my reduced circumstances but Spike was respectful and did what he could.

"Sorry, Johnny, all we've got right now are catering jobs."

"Dinna worry, Spike, I've done worse."

"Right. Kitchen Porter. Marcliffe Hotel. £11 per week, hours variable."

"I'll take it, give me the card."

Spike handed me the vacancy card with the contact details and I headed up to Queen's Terrace. From many visits to the Marcliffe mainly on Sunday nights for the famous performances by the legendary folk band "Hedgehog Pie," I knew my way around the place and quickly found Raymond Brown, the trainee Restaurant Manager, who seemed happy to find a job applicant. He took me to my new place of work, explaining that the previous Kitchen Porter had "gone mental" and disappeared off the face of the earth two days before, leaving the rest of the staff to try and cope with his duties.

These comprised washing the pots and utensils, removing the rubbish and mopping the floor, not exceptionally demanding on any intellectual level but fairly arduous on a physical level. As this was something to which I had no earlier exposure, I relished the novelty and got stuck into two days' backlog of sticky pans and various whisks and rollers. The Chef religiously cleaned his own knives so the only real danger came from the boiling water and the increasingly slippy floor. I was constantly reminded in quaintly industrial language to keep sweeping, mopping and shifting the detritus to the bins outside. By lunchtime we had cleared the breakfast backlog and got completely up to snuff by three o'clock.

Chef made us a sandwich from the leftovers; we all had a cup of tea and a read of the daily papers, patting each other on the back and swapping the usual stories. There was a two-hour break before returning for the Teatime session, which ran into Dinner and no interruptions until everything had been washed, scrubbed and stowed away for the next day by about 9.45pm. The Bar closed at ten in those days, so the Chef made sure we all had a drink ordered before we closed up. He scrambled up some more delicious leftovers washed down with a well-deserved pint of lager. This was a pleasing end to an unexpectedly enjoyable working session and I looked forward to the next day.

My next day's stint started at 11am, which gave me plenty time to stumble out of bed and stroll round the corner from the flat in Holburn Street that I shared with my younger brother. The day followed a similar pattern but since there was less of a backlog we got through the chores a bit earlier and, therefore, had a longer break in the afternoon. I was getting into a reasonable rhythm and began to reason that this might not be such a bad job after all. Free scoff, a read of the papers and a pint at the end of the day. What more did a person need?

What I did not need was Raymond Brown suddenly announcing that the previous incumbent had returned to the planet, got his head "together" and wanted his job back. There was nothing I could do. For my efforts I got a steak sandwich, an *Evening Express,* a pint, a fiver and an apologetic thank you and headed back, disconsolately, to Holburn Street.

Next day it was back to Market Street, where the ever sympathetic Spike advised me that there were no other jobs but consoled me with the thought that as I had been effectively "sacked" rather than walking off the job, I would now qualify for unemployment benefit, which I could expect after a bit of form filling and a wait of a few more weeks. I remember filling in the forms and leaving them with Spike to process. By extremely good fortune on my way out of the "Broo" I bumped into Jim Simpson.

"Hullo, young Johnny."

"Fit like, Jimmy?"

To all his family and old friends he was known as "Jimmy" much in the same way that to all the people that I had met before attaining the age of twenty I was known as "Johnny." To all his business associates and for the purposes of this tale his name is "Jim." This will also be useful in distinguishing between him and Jimmy Gallan. It is axiomatic that, in determination of who is "Jim" and who is "Jimmy" the Rule of Height shall apply. The Simpson James was a reasonably tall five foot ten and the Gallan version only five foot seven and so I hope the reader will be able to follow the "Jim" and "Jimmy" dichotomy.

"What are you up to these days? I haven't seen you since you and Alex helped us out with the barytes last year. Have you finished your degree yet?"

Jim was genuinely curious and unfailingly polite. I was definitely gauche in comparison but managed to get across that I had not managed to complete the course and was looking for work to fill in my "gap year".

"Ony jobs, Jimmy?"

"Well, as it happens, I am on the lookout for a Customs Clerk to do a bit of stock control, but that would only be part-time, how good is your counting?"

"I'm a mathematical genius!"

I repeated the hyperbolic response given to Jimmy Gallan the previous year when faced with the same question, comfortable in the knowledge that Jim Simpson always preferred self-confidence and overstatement to false humility. This view was formed in my mind from only a few previous encounters.

Jim looked like a respectable gangster with his tanned features, carefully cut mohair suits, tailored shirts, cufflinks, silk tie, shiny loafers and a Benson & Hedges invariably to hand. He always spoke well with an extensive vocabulary and he had a keen ear for a novel turn of phrase with which he could embellish his wide range of anecdotes. He was knowledgeable about The Arts but not drawn to pretension or intellectualism, preferring Kitsch to Nietsche and Boogie Woogie to Beethoven. This was reflected in his choice of automobiles. When I had last met him he drove a "Yank Tank," a 1963 Chevrolet Impala, electric blue with massive white fins, a "left hooker" with a knob on the steering wheel to help guide the beast around Aberdeen's twisty roads. Having recently acquired a yellow Alfa Romeo Giuletta, the epitome of Sixties Cool, Jim was now about to change it for the brand new Jaguar XJ6. He would later swap that for a Saluki Bronze Citroen Maserati SM before acquiring his infamous Lincoln Continental Coupe in stunning black. You are what you drive.

Jim outlined the present situation with "The Service Company." After three years of intermittent activity there was now a steady flow of material (Dubs) in and out of his Regent Road premises. Some other competitors had moved in but he had a queue of prospective clients preferring to use his facilities. Gordon Graham was in the final throes of being wound up and Jim was going to concentrate all his attentions thenceforth to ASC. Jimmy Gallan now had a full-time crew of helpers and there had been a few new acquisitions in plant and equipment. He was upgrading office accommodation within the warehouse and would soon be looking for office staff. He had an old fellow working part time looking after the stock control records but this chap had been struggling with the physical demands of getting about the sacks and pallets and, anyway, was due to retire.

"It's not much of a job and only £6 a week for 20 hours. It might keep you going until you get back to University. Come and have a look see."

We climbed into his Alfa Romeo and skited along the cobbled streets of the harbour towards Regent Road. While Jim strained to find a parking place I looked around and noted only a few minor changes to the familiar surroundings. We walked down the lane toward the office where Jim collared Danny Gibb, the joiner, as he was putting the finishing touches to a door on the new glass-fronted block in the far corner.

"Aye, aye, Danny when's my office going to be ready? You've been on it for months now. I'll need to be moving in next week."

"Eh! Eh! Eh!" Danny stammered. He was not a quick thinker, though he was fairly quick at finding excuses. "But ye said ye wantit a Quality Job so ye'll jist hiv tae wait! I've still tae dae the panellin an the lichts an at'll need a Sparkie."

"Pah!" Jim scoffed. "Noah built his Ark in less time."

Danny banged his hammer into a four-inch nail, muffling his disrespectful reply. Jim Simpson was no slave driver but he did try to transmit a sense of urgency. Danny the joiner was recently retired

29

and ever on the look out to pick up jobs for "beer money." He liked to plead poverty and claim that he needed the money for subsistence. More importantly he needed the companionship that came from the working life as he had recently lost his wife. Jim Simpson, even with his hard cynical outward self, was often a sucker for hard luck stories and had engaged Danny at the suggestion of a mutual friend at the RUA Club (where obligations were held religiously.)

We moved on to the "bothy" where we found Jimmy Gallan drinking his tea along with a few other familiar faces eating their "pieces." As the pace of business had picked up Jimmy had acquired a squad of full-time workers to help with the lifting and loading, bagging and bulking, driving and dumping and all tasks associated with the mud handling and storage. It was obvious from the names and faces that Jimmy had applied his own particular selection criteria in picking his new team. Jimmy's Team was packed with the cream of the hard working and reliable "Country Boys" rather than "The Toonsers" from the old Gordon Graham gang. I recognised Bob Allan but did not know Jock Begg, Jake Morrison and Sandy Scott. These guys hailed from Kinellar and Kintore rather than Kincorth. From my previous short stint at cutting barytes I knew that this was a tough job and could see straight away that these guys were fit and capable. Jim Simpson had also added a couple of his own "picks"—his half brother, Richard Forbes and his cousin, Norman Simpson. They had not, as far as I knew, had any experience of working with "Dubs" and it proved interesting watching them cope with it.

Jim took me into the old office and introduced me to Bill Fraser, a short stocky fellow with a toothbrush moustache, horn rimmed glasses, a well worn striped suit, military tie and various bits of Freemasonry Regalia. Bill was obviously another RUA secondee. I knew from Jim Simpson's account that I was being lined up to help Bill with his stock control duties and reasoned that I would have to be prepared to get on with him on a business level; however, I knew straight off the bat that I was going to have some difficulties on any kind of social level.

Within only a few minutes he had made derisory comments about my hair, my clothes and my University career. This put me on the defensive but, in the few short months that we, subsequently, managed to share an office, I heard him say much worse things about women, foreigners, shirkers, Unions, government officials and just about everybody else. It is probably just as well he wasn't there to witness the influx of various nationalities and, more importantly, the revolutionary wave of working principles and practices that was to sweep through Regent Road and Aberdeen from 1971 onwards.

During our discussion Jim Simpson mentioned that Shell had asked him if The Service Company could provide a Customs Clerk on a part time basis to compile Bonded Warehouse documents and other minor duties. With his usual courtesy he offered this first to Bill, who had experience of completing the same documents for Number 5 Bond. Whether this task was perceived as *infra dig* or whether he was displaying rare magnanimity, Bill declined the opportunity and suggested that "The Laddie" (me) might be able to take this on as a way of learning the ropes. Of course I jumped at the chance and arrangements were made for me to call at 244 Market Street on Monday 1st June 1970 and report to a Mr. John Snodgrass.

"Snodgrass?" I queried, evoking an image of the character in the "Beachcomber" column of the Daily Express. I figured that Jim shared my appreciation of Goonish humour.

"Aye, Snodgrass," Jim smirked and cautioned, "But let's nae tak' the piss oot o' the customer – at least until they've paid the bill!"

The job at Shell was a "shoe in." Although I was desperate for a job, Shell were equally anxious to have someone to perform the mundane task of filling in Customs forms and Jim Simpson was very keen to get his foot in the door at Shell. Up to that point, since coming to Aberdeen in 1965, Shell had been almost self-sufficient in staffing terms and Jim wanted to be involved in the parts of this business that were much more exciting (and profitable) than cutting barytes. The £44 per month paid by Shell almost covered my wages and I was relieved that I would be at least paying my way. The Shell work was scheduled for Monday and Thursday mornings. The other mornings I was due to share with Bill Fraser in the Regent Road office learning the ropes on keeping the stock records for the mud company clients.

Let me describe that office so that you can understand my claustrophobic feelings about the place. It was a "lean-to" construction located in the corner of the old beer store, devoid of natural daylight and with no ventilation. From the entrance to the rear wall it measured about fifteen feet and was no more than eight feet wide and seven foot high. The walls were made of recycled wood to waist height with glass panels reaching to the ceiling. The ceiling was chipboard, painted white with a double fluorescent lamp fixture. In front of the painted stone wall there was one of Gordon Graham's surplus desks and an old green filing cabinet.

On a shelf alongside sat an array of telephones, which, in a more salubrious environment, might have looked impressive, as they were all different colours. In the Sixties we had progressed from the old standard black bakelite handsets. The Post Office, which had the monopoly on the telephone system, would give you, included in the £8 per quarter line rental fee, a not too impressive choice of a regulation grey/beige combination or (for an extra £2 per quarter) a solid colour option in red, green or blue. Black or white phones seemed to be reserved for dignitaries, celebrities and plutocrats so, obviously, must have been too expensive for mere mortals (and Aberdeen Service Company) to consider.

There was room available for only two cheap plastic visitors chairs and a tiny cupboard containing the office essentials—Tea, Coffee, Sugar and Milk. This, therefore was not, by any means a modern, ergonomically designed office as you would expect from a place which proved to be in 1970/1971 the epicentre of a blossoming international industry that prevented Britain from going down the tubes.

Add to this, Dear Reader, the effect of Bill Fraser chain smoking his Woodbines, swilling his rum-laced coffee and ranting on about "The War," Communist Plots, Women's Libbers and Poofs and you will understand why I spent most of my time roving the warehouse and the other parts of the derelict grain mill that comprised No. 5 Bond.

On my regular tours, ostensibly checking the sack count of Walnut Plug or RD-333 or to verify the amounts recorded on the Kardex stock cards, I would be collared by the Gaffer.

"Hemmin, haud that ere the Bobby comes!"

Jimmy would shout as he passed by on the forklift pointing to a bag of Flosal or Mica Coarse that would invariably be dislodged from a stowed pallet as it was being steered along the undulating cobbled floor.

"We'll need to re-stow this lot. Gie's a haun. Damn shoogly stuff. Here, how d'ye fancy workin for a livin instead o wanderin aboot wi a pencil? We've twa hunner ton o barytes an a hunner ton o cement tae cut afore Midnight an we're half a man short."

I took the faintly insulting invitation as a compliment and did not have to hide my enthusiasm. The deeper, more complicated wells encountered in the Northern Sector with greater depths and higher operating pressures had led to an unprecedented demand for "Dubs" and Jimmy's crew had been stretched to the limit, so I was roped into Jimmy's Team to help out as a general labourer. This proved to be not too unbearable as I was reasonably fit, had nothing better to fill my time and desperately needed the money.

Jimmy had already worked out the division of labour. The two Jocks were the strongest and were put on the "front line" lifting and cutting. Sandy Scott was smaller and slighter but had proven a nifty forklift driver and was given that role. Richard and Norman were deemed to be less physical and were sidelined to driving the Bulker. As I could not yet drive a lorry or a forklift I was assigned to a variety of duties from straightening pallets, to climbing up on to the bulker, hanging from the top hatch rim and kicking the powdered cement and barytes towards the corners in order to maximise and balance the load.

All these "skills" were lost when we eventually found a warehouse with a level floor and eliminated altogether when CEBO arrived (in 1972) with their fully automated bulk plant and 350 Ton silos refurbished from seaborne tankers that carried 5000 Tons per shipment. Until these developments arrived The Service Company had to get by with brute strength and a great deal of ingenuity. During the summer and autumn of 1970 we must have shifted about 10,000 tons of barytes, cement, bentonite and salt. We worked evenings and weekends and sometimes through the night in order to keep up with demand.

There was one occasion when Jimmy Gallan left his home in Holburn Road as usual at 7am on a Thursday and did not return until Teatime on the Saturday (paypacket intact.) We dragged in all sorts of temporary help. Richard called in Bill Burnett, Hebbie Spence (our new Mechanic) press-ganged Colin Fraser and Jock Smith roped in his old trawlerman sidekick John Watt and several others. It was no surprise that there was a fair turnover in the "casuals."

This was arduous effort in a very poor environment with a high safety risk. What is more surprising, in hindsight, is how many of those who came to help stayed the course for a fixed rate of ten shillings (fifty pence) per hour. Some were qualified tradesmen, some had full-time jobs elsewhere, some had gambling debts; but all appreciated that, in general, jobs in Aberdeen were hard to find, poorly paid and not secure, so an extra Ten Bob an Hour (especially Tax Free) was welcome. If the Taxman feels the urge to follow up on this unpaid tax I would caution them to save their breath as all the people mentioned are either dead or living overseas on the wealth they (subsequently) created as a result of being given this healthy introduction to the Global Oil Business.

By December 1970 I had been established as Aberdeen Service Company's first full time office employee. Bill Fraser had retired and I had taken on the stock control function as well as the Customs paperwork. As I still had to help out in various warehouse duties Jim Simpson spotted the need to have someone to answer the phones and greet the growing swell of business visitors and nosey-parkers coming to see what was all the fuss about this North Sea Oil. He drafted in the vivacious Pat Morrison who had been the Receptionist at Gordon Graham.

Before we became internationalised and made Christmas Day the major holiday event, we Aberdonians clung to the Presbyterian idea that a single day off was all that was required for our winter festival. That day was New Year's Day and on the 31st December 1970 after a year of hard work and successful trading the boys at The Service Company were given a little bonus of an extra week's wages (About £15) in their pay packet. At just after one o'clock Pat handed out the eagerly expected brown envelopes with her usual cheery smile. Jimmy Gallan also announced that, as everything was up to date, everybody could enjoy a rare treat of finishing early and well before two o'clock the place was deserted, as workers and wages sped off home or to the pub. Pat was putting on her coat when the blue "Baroid" phone rang. On the line was John Spargo, the Hamilton Brothers representative. As the discussion passed to technical matters Pat handed the call to Jimmy and headed for the door. Smiling at first Jimmy nodded, hummed, ha'd and made his normal accommodating remarks before hanging up.

"Damn the bit!"

Jimmy fumed, absorbing the fact that he had just agreed to something that was going to prove difficult, if not impossible, to achieve. His look told me that I could not expect to enjoy the afternoon off.

"Spargo needs a hunner and fifty ton o brine on the *Smit Lloyd 3* by midnight. It's Hogmanay and I've jist let a'body ging hame. Richt, we'll jist hiv tae get them back. But, haud on, it'll be at least an oor afore the "country" boys get hame an the "toonsers" will, nae doubt, be in some pub spendin their bonus afore the wife gets a hauds o them. Right, you, get on yer b'iler suit, open up the sack store an see foo muckle we've gotten. I'll phone aroon an see if I can get ane or twa mair tae help us."

As I had made no plans for Hogmanay, other than a promise

to meet my mates in the Silver Slipper at seven, I jumped at the command, donned my blue nylon boiler suit, grabbed the keys and headed for the sack store. I knew that 150 tons of brine would require 30 pallets of salt and 3 pallets of chromate. We had mixed lots of this during the year but never in any kind of hurry.

Normally this would require two men at the sack store and four at Pocra Quay where Baroid had their Brine Tank. When I returned to confirm to Jimmy that we had sufficient stock I was relieved to hear that he had managed to get some extra help. Richard Forbes was not a drinking man and, as he lived nearby, had agreed to come back. Nobody else could be reached. Jimmy was straight into his plan of action. He would work the Climax forklift and load the Commer truck. Richard would drive. I was to take the Henly Hawk from Regent Road to Pocra Quay in readiness for the first load. During my various stints in the store I had been given "shotties" at steering and parking the forklift but had never driven on the open road.

"I'm nae sure if I can handle that thing on the road," I pleaded.

"That's a' richt," said Jimmy, dismissing my concern. "It's an automatic, it'll steer itsel'."

"But, Jimmy, I hivnae got a licence."

"Nivver heed. If a Bobby stops ye jist tell 'im ye're lost. If ye hivnae got a licence he canna tak it aff ye."

Following this irrefutable logic and in appreciation of the urgency, I took the keys to the Hawk, jumped aboard, switched on the headlamps, lifted the forks and headed for Pocra Quay. By the time I reached there, Richard was arriving with the first load of salt. Jimmy had also come to prime the loading hose and fill the tank. He siphoned the fresh water from the River Dee and had the flow going by the time that we had offloaded the first pallet. Richard and I climbed on to the work platform and started cutting the sacks in the same manner as I imagine a fisherman would gut a cod or similar sized beast. Manhandling 50kilo sacks while wielding a gutting knife could be risky but, as we had done this a few times before, we were coping comfortably. Jimmy took the Commer back

36

to the sack-store to collect the second load. We had emptied five or six pallets by the time he returned.

At about the same time the Baroid man, Bob Pate, had appeared. Bob was a tall, gangling American, droll in his manner and slightly awkward in his movements. I guess that is how he acquired his nickname of "Tanglefoot". As he had only recently arrived in Aberdeen we had not yet had a chance to get to know him. I think he had been sitting happily in the Lounge Bar at The Marcliffe when the "grapevine" got the message to him that his customer, Hamilton Brothers, had placed this urgent order. As an able and qualified Mud Engineer he appreciated the technical intricacies as well as the commercial importance and had hightailed it down to the dockside along with his Mud Balance Kit to ensure that we would mix the salt and sodium chromate to the required Specific Gravity (SG).

"Who's ramroddin' this bunch?" Bob asked the Ship's Mate, who was at the gangway of the *Smit Lloyd 3* watching all that was going on.

"There's your man," the Dutchman said in impeccable English, pointing to the small figure in blue coveralls and black beret, ferociously ferreting about the hose and pipe connections on his vessel.

"You must be Jim Gallan." Bob greeted the figure emerging from the bowels of the *SL3*.

"Aye, that's me and you'll be Joe's new sidekick. Are ye here tae help or hinder?"

Joe Whittlesey had set up the Baroid Aberdeen office and must have alerted Bob to Jimmy Gallan's capabilities as well as his sense of humour. Bob picked up on the friendly banter and introduced himself to Richard and myself before going on to explain that Hamilton had asked for a very precise mix and SG for this order and that he would be there to make sure that everything met the strict specification before the boat sailed. He had been told of the significance of the Scottish Hogmanay and was genuinely impressed that The Service Company had managed to respond to the emergency.

In the true spirit of cooperation he hauled his gangly frame up to the platform to help out with the sack handling, (Just like wrasslin' alligators,) or worked the gun-type agitators used for stirring up the sediment (Just like makin' Gumbo.) He also fetched the fish suppers, which proved a welcome warmer on the frosty night. No extra salt required. This also proved to be a rare exception to Bob's usual parsimony. As Jimmy summed up when later asked for his estimation of Bob Pate: "He's that tight, he could peel an orange in his trooser pocket!"

We finished the third and final tank-load about 8pm, Bob verified the SG, Jimmy and Richard looked after the transfer to the vessel and the tidying up of pallets, sacks and hoses while I took the forklift back along the deserted harbour roads to the sack store. By the time I had returned and changed out of my soaking, salt encrusted coveralls, the others had caught me up. Richard locked up and Jimmy gave me a lift back to my flat. It did not take me long to get washed and changed into my "going out" gear.

After a quick dash through the back streets I made it to the Silver Slipper where my chums had been drinking merrily since seven. It was now 9.30, the Bar was due to close at 10 and I was in need of a well earned pint, but my friends' curiosity was aroused by my weather-beaten features and shortage of breath.

"Far hiv you been, Johnny, ye're lookin hashed!"

As succinctly as I could I explained that I had been helping to prepare and despatch 150 tons of brine on a boat destined for the North Sea. They were incredulous to a man.

"A hunner an' fifty ton o' salt water? Tae the North Sea? Fit kin' o' dope hiv ye been smokin' tae come up a story like that?"

# 3. Damn Toon Dirt

Aberdeen began to become aware of environmental and ecological issues as far back as 1971. As well as the more widely publicised rants from the Hippies and Yippies there had been some informed warnings from sound-minded scientists at The Torry Marine Lab on conservation of fishing prospects and from The Rowett Institute on the effects of nitrates and other pollutants on feedwater stocks. I had always been extremely careful with the meagre share of Earth's resources that fell into my lap, always finishing every morsel of food on my plate, rinsing and re-cycling every glass bottle (especially if there was a refundable threepence deposit,) using the blank pages of any book for sketching and scribbling but never, ever, dropping litter in the streets. As I had not spent much time in rural areas I was not too aware of The Country Code although I did attain my Wayfarers Badge at the Boys Brigade and would certainly try to be mindful of my responsibilities to Nature's Parlour if I ever received the opportunity to visit.

I remember being impressed by an article written in The Observer around Autumn 1968 by Des Wilson, the buck-toothed New Zealander who went on to become the official spokesman for the Liberals on environmental issues. The Observer was not my regular Sunday Paper but there had been a special supplement of Snoopy Cartoons so I bought it and, not wishing to waste paper and gain full value for the ninepence invested, I had proceeded with reading the full publication.

Des Wilson wrote in language I could understand about the seminal subjects of Earth's diminishing resources, particularly fossil fuels, problems with waste disposal, especially nuclear matter and the inexorable effects of fuel consumption arising from increasing surface and air transportation. This was an illuminating article which fed my fertile imagination and might have caused

39

me to fret about mankind's long-term existence on our planet had I not been more concerned about my own short-term survival, which at that time was calculated on a week to week basis. Des also touched on the dangers of urban sprawl and the associated dangers of contaminated landfill and it all seemed cogent and quite worrying.

I had also taken in one of the world famous BBC Reith Lectures delivered by Lord Ritchie Calder. This was not by choice but essentially the only entertainment available one cold evening in November 1969, when I was stuck at home alone in our student "pad" at 1 Devanha Terrace, lights out, meter empty, pockets empty, waiting for the return of my flatmates (who had gone back to their Ma's for food and laundry service.) I tuned my battery-powered transistor into the only available Radio Station—The Home Service (cruel irony, there.) Ritchie Calder had been wittering on for years about the apocalyptic effects of over-population, despoliation of nature, dehumanisation and all sorts of things foretold by Voltaire, Malthus, Veblen et al. Much of this futuristic philosophy was ignored by most levels of society but was attracting attention from the weirder wings of the populace. It was regarded as hokum back then, as it had been for centuries previously, but strangely seems to be the hot topic nowadays.

All this was vaguely in my mind as were preparing a " richt guid redd oot" at the Coal Hole early in 1971. Space, as always, was at a premium and, even with the high turnover of stock, there never seemed to be enough room to store the hundreds of pallets of sacks and drums of valuable ingredients of drilling mud.

With the increased activity in offshore drilling most of the items would be rotated within weeks or even a few days, but there were some old barrels and bags that had been lying about for years and they were beginning to show signs of deterioration, a bit of rust on the metal drums and the odd tear in the paper sacks.

Disposing of the waste sacks from the regular bulk cutting operations had been routine; after a spell of splitting the sacks of barytes, bentonite, cement or salt and decanting their contents into bulkers, silos or brine tanks, we would bundle up the torn paper into sheaves, load them on to a flatbed and haul the lot to the Municipal Tip where we would manhandle everything on to the piles of builders' rubble and household refuse that comprised the local dump. There had never been any problem with this until the rabid scaremongering of the more enthusiastic environmentalists, highlighted by the activities of Greenpeace and Friends of the Earth, provoked the Media to run lurid feature articles in the broadsheets and show TV programmes about some unscrupulous industrialists sneaking their toxic waste on to landfill sites, causing our babies to be deformed and our dolphins to die horrible deaths. One of our caring, sharing Councillors must have been watching a Panorama Special on his monochrome Ferguson seventeen-inch and, sharing the anxiety that hitherto had been the preserve of eighteenth century philosophers, passed on his concerns to the Management and thenceforth to the operatives at the Girdleness Depot.

I cast my mind back to an earlier occasion on a routine trip to our local Dump. Jock Smith trundled the flatbed Ford through the gates into the tip. Jock was normally assigned to drive the Ford (as it was nearly knackered already) and was usually charged with the "recycling" duties. He had the inside track on the best places to sell scrap and dump the debris and it kept him away from doing more damage to our more valuable pieces of kit back at Regent Road. I was second man as usual, as I had nothing better to do. We had a load of empty barytes sacks on board as per normal after cutting a hundred ton of bulk the previous day and were preparing to add them to the other rubbish rapidly filling the disused granite quarry that was Aberdeen's biggest tip at the time. The Depot Supervisor approached. He had a clipboard, therefore he was a Supervisor. Natch!

"Fit's 'at?"

"Fit's fit?" Jock responded.

"That stuff on your lorry, in the paper sacks. Fit is it?"

"It's barytes, fit wye are ye askin?"

"Ye canna dump 'at here!"

41

"Fit wye nae? We've been dumpin it here for years. Fit's yer problem?"

"We've been tellt tae look out for Toxic Waste, especially fae you big oil types!"

"Awayaraj! There's naethin toxic aboot it. You tell him, Brains!"

We hardly looked like "Big Oil" types, in our dust covered boiler suits, with a truckload of torn paper sacks aboard our beat up Ford, but this was obviously a man on a mission. I could see as he reached for his new red Biro that he meant business. I could also see from Jock's pulsating neck and the colour of his complexion that our local Jobsworth might end with something more than red ink on his clipboard if we carried on with this tack and I offered my explanation that this was Barium Sulphate, a totally inert clay salt and of no danger to any living creature.

Making notes in fairly neat (but not "joined up") writing the Supervisor asked me to spell everything out to which I responded as intelligibly and politely as I could. He enquired how I knew all this stuff and I countered that I had an "A" Level in Chemistry (which I have) and he looked querulously as to how someone with proper paper qualifications could be riding shotgun on a dilapidated dumper with a load of waste paper and mud on a freezing February afternoon. I wondered that myself but I, too, had a wage to earn. When he had finished writing he grudgingly nodded his assent and told us where to dump our cargo. This did not correspond with where Jock wanted to put it but, as darkness approached, we did not want to prolong the issue.

After we had tipped our load and were heading for the exit our new best friend stopped us again and offered us the information that, owing to some sort of world shortage of raw material, he had heard how Davidson's the Paper Merchant was paying £5 per ton for waste paper. Jock said nothing, thumped his heavy left boot on the clutch, grabbed the selection lever, crunched it into a gear at random, thundered the throttle and lurched off through the gates. He did not utter a word until we had reached the lighthouse on the coast road.

"Could the bastard nae hiv telt us that afore we startit?"

We had learned two things from our trip to the tip. We would no longer be allowed to dump our waste willy-nilly and we now had a much more worthwhile outlet for our plentiful supply of paper. Although we used the jobsworth's advice on the waste paper to our considerable benefit (for full details read Chapter 7 on the "Barytes Cutters Ball") we had to be a lot more careful about dumping the other debris. Jimmy Gallan was waiting for us when we returned.

"Ye're awa an awfu lang time. Did ye get tint?"

"Naw, we were nae lost," Jock replied "The Cooncil mannie widna let us dump the secks. He wintit tae ken if barytes wis some kinna pusion but "Brains" sorted him oot."

We set to thinking what we would do with rest of the material that had to be dumped. If we were to be hassled on the barytes then we could expect major problems with the other items. We were loosely aware of the properties of the chemicals that we had been handling and had been assured by people we could trust that there was nothing particularly harmful. We had always taken extra care in handling the metal drums and plastic bags containing Caustic Soda as it could burn a bit. Likewise with Flosal, a kind of Asbestos, for though we had been told that it was a benign form, we always used face-masks when handling it.

The Mud Companies were notoriously secretive about the contents and properties of their proprietary products and did not advertise the ingredients lest their competitors would discover their trade secrets.

It was in my role as Customs Clerk that I managed to learn a little more about the mystical properties of the compounds and potions that our clients had been purveying. As some of the products being disposed of had been manufactured overseas they had been imported under HM Customs & Excise Bonded Warehouse Regulations. In order to be scrapped they had to be diverted to "Home Use" which involved form filling and inspection. Our local Customs Inspector was the amiable Walter Burnett. Walter was no Jobsworth but he did have a natural curiosity and he insisted on knowing more about the chemicals before he approved for disposal.

In order to complete the Customs paperwork I had to consult the Mud Engineering Technical Manuals. Even my Chemistry A Level had not prepared me for this so I had the pleasure of working with John Schofield, a recent arrival to the IMC ranks. John had earned a Degree in Chemical Engineering, which exempted him from the usual three month Mud School. He was tall with a muscular build and, having grown up on a farm, could handle himself in a hard working environment. On more than one occasion he joined in helping us with our bulk cutting operations. With his brains, brawn and generosity of spirit it was only his accent that betrayed his Yorkshire origins.

We discovered no major revelations in what constituted the ingredients of the mud sacks and drums. "RD-333" for example, sounded like a magical compound when described as a "Superior Bonding Agent," and selling for £25 per fifty-pound sack. In fact it turned out to be dried, powdered quebracho resin. "Quebracho" sounded fairly exotic, too, until I discovered it was nothing more than tree-bark. "CMC" was another sinister sounding bonding agent but merely represented the initials of the formula for Carboxy Methyl Cellulose. John divulged to me that this was similar to wallpaper paste. IMC's customers, the oil companies who paid for this mundane mixer, were happy to part with £30 for each 25kg sack of CMC.

They paid a heck of a lot more for "Pipe-Free," fetching over £900 per 45 Gallon Drum. There was one of these drums that must have been lying about our warehouse for a few years (and probably a few years in Yarmouth before that) as the steel casing was visibly corroding and the label was almost indistinguishable. From a purely commercial viewpoint it would have been difficult to persuade a client, even one as well-heeled as Amoco, to part with all that dosh for shop-soiled goods.

In determining the correct Customs Tariff Code for the "Pipe

44

Free" I had to ask some pertinent questions to my IMC collaborator as to the make-up of this drum of luxury liquid but I found he was being unusually unforthcoming. It must have related to the seemingly extortionate selling price and John's undoubted loyalty to his employer that I found difficulty in extricating the truth; it turned out that "Pipe Free" was little more than household detergent with a few hydrocarbon enhancements. As the name implies, it was designed to be added to the fluids in the wellbore when the drill string became jammed in the rock formation and aid the lubrication of the sticking points to free the pipe.

Such situations were rare however, but given the huge day rates for offshore drilling rigs and the costs associated with "down time" on stuck pipe, the client was prepared to pay premium rates to obtain a product that would minimise losses. This was a classic supply and demand issue. No price gouging—honest!

With the recent experience of the man with the red biro at the local dump fresh in my mind I, asked the IMC man if we should take special precautions in disposing of the Pipe Free. He merely shook his head and said he would be happy to have it dumped on his own family farm and that it would do no harm to man nor beast; in fact it might help to break up the boulder clay soil. As a Yorkshireman he was reluctant to toss away nine hundred quid of potential profit but he was learning the ways of his new masters and coming to terms with Global Economics. I got all the information I needed, added the Tariff Codes to the Customs Forms and took them across the Swing Bridge to Walter Burnett's office on Regent Quay for rubber-stamping. Some of the antiquated document transfers were quicker than email and I was back at the Coal Hole before Jock had finished his morning tea and rowies.

Walter Burnett, conscientious to a fault, accompanied me and ensured the drums being disposed of were damaged beyond commercial redemption. At his insistence we banged a chisel into the lid and made sure that this product was fit only for the dump. With the preliminaries over we loaded the burst drums and torn sacks on to the Commer (the Ford flatbed was in for repair with a gearbox problem) and prepared to head to the tip. Jimmy had remembered the previous escapade at Girdleness and suggested we take this cargo to the private dump further out at Marywell. Even though this tip was further away and would incur a £2 tipping fee he reckoned it would be quicker and cheaper. He handed Jock the money and gave his instructions and we went on our way. I donned my blue boiler suit and climbed into the passenger seat.

As we sashayed along the granite setts of Market Street, Jock's tuneless whistling matching the whine of the Commer's transmission, I estimated we were carrying about £5000 worth of redundant chemicals on the back of our wagon. This must be quite a business, I mused, where companies could throw away this amount of money. As we drove past my birthplace in Menzies Road I calculated that the load of powders and potions on the back of our lorry was worth more than an entire block of the tenement flats that had been home to many in my direct family over the years. Scary statistic! In the course of the next thirty years I came to appreciate that this was but a drop in the ocean for the oil companies and, somewhere along the line, house prices have caught up.

We scooted past Craiginches and Kincorth and out into the green countryside with nothing but prefabs and caravans to block our view of the desolate heathland that is now known, quaintly, as Grampian Country Park. As I drive, nowadays, along the sweeping dual carriageway of Wellington Road past the vainglorious showrooms of the self-important car dealers and the burgeoning blocks of offices, typified by the ridiculous "Chocolate Box" that Shell developed as its North Sea Headquarters, I wonder whether we might still have been so critical of our jobs, our lifestyle, our housing and even our football team, had it not been for the efforts of those early pioneers, Jock included, who made sure that the fundamental shorebased jobs were done in support of the vital offshore drilling that led to the North Sea Bonanza.

Time slows down in the countryside. It's true! "Town" time is quicker, "City" time even slicker and, as we know, a New York Minute is but a bat of a neurotic bat's eyelid. It could not have been more than five minutes since we passed the Nigg Post Office and headed past Loch Loirston towards Marywell, approaching the private dump to which Jimmy Gallan had sent us.

In "Country" time it seemed like hours and, when we reached the drive, we felt that we had stepped back into an earlier timezone. During the Sixties, Grampian TV had run a popular programme called "Bothy Nichts" in which all sorts of amateur entertainers and unrestrained show-offs such as "The Angus Cronies," and "The Kennethmont Loons and Quines," had caricatured their agricultural predecessors, reciting incomprehensible monologues, poems and cornkister jokes, singing familiar but clichéd ballads and, generally, acting like gypes. We all laughed at the anachronisms and the affected accents, as did my Granny Aggie and Auld Jake, her younger brother, who had grown up in Kennethmont but could not recall having had much time for such revelry after a hard day in the field or in Service at Keith Hall. The character standing by the gate of the dump was no caricature. From the bottom of his tackety boots to the top of his bunnit, from his calloused hand to the bright red point on the nose of his weather-beaten face he was obviously of authentic agricultural stock. His rich Doric brogue confirmed it.

Although we must have been no more than five miles from the city we could have been in a foreign country for all that I could understand of the verbal exchanges. Jock appeared to fare little better and had resorted to sign language in asking for and receiving directions as to where to drop our cargo of damaged dubs. We drove over to the side of a quarry to dump the pallets of powdered material but were directed to the broken down byre to offload the barrels. As there was no forklift or other handling device we proceeded to push the drums off the side of the Commer. As they tumbled on to the rocky, bumpy surface the contents of the "Pipe Free" spewed out of the holes that our Customs Inspector had insisted on. I imagined we had dropped one on to the gatekeeper's toes as he let out a yell. I understood the first part of his expletive as it was a term used commonly by Jimmy Gallan when faced with local incompetents.

"Damn toon dirt . . .!" We heard him shout.

"Fit's wrang? Are ye a' right?"

We could see he was unhurt but might have become spattered by some of the fluid that continued to gurgle from the barrel. There was a strange aroma that probably emanated from the small amount of hydrocarbons that had been added to the basic detergent and I surmised that our incomprehensible gatekeeper might be concerned about the possible pollutant effects of this compound. As he reiterated the expletive he added a few more words that I failed to interpret. In an attempt to assuage his temper I tried to tell him that this was no more than washing up liquid and that our expert chemist John Schofield had affirmed that he would have been happy to have it dumped on his own father's farm. There was no calming down our local yokel however, and with more ranting and frantic hand gestures he directed us to raise the drum to an upright position. Jock and I did as we were bid and looked at each other hoping that he was not going to ask us to lift it back on to the lorry and, thankfully, he said no more other than to indicate that we should pay the £2 dumping charge before getting on our way. That much we did manage to understand. We paid the money, climbed back on board and beat a hasty retreat.

On our way out we heard him utter his now familiar catchphrase and I asked Jock what he thought was irking our gatekeeper. In between banging pedals and crashing gears Jock responded that the "Teuchter" (everybody in the city refers, erroneously, to country dwellers as Teuchters just as the rural dwellers refer to us as "Toonsers") had probably presumed that the drums contained some sort of oil that could be used as fuel for heating his cowshed or for boiling his pigswill and was disappointed when we had spilled some of the valuable contents.

In Jock's view everybody operated on some sort of buckshee basis and Teuchters were no different from Toonsers in that regard. If, indeed, our farmer friend was hoping to use the drum as fuel it was probably just as well that we would be well out of earshot by the time he got round to trying to ignite it. In my naivety I believed that our country cousins had more consideration for the sanctity of the environment and, on our return to Regent Road, I canvassed the view of Jimmy Gallan.

"Here, Jimmy, we got rid o' the stuff but I dinna think oor man at the dump was awfa pleased. I dinna ken a' that he said but he kept using thon expression o' yours."

"Fit ane's that then?"

"Damn Toon Dirt!" I said.

"Aye, ye're a' that, as sure's a cat's a hairy beast."

"But he went on and rantit mair. Fit wis 'e tryin' tae tell us, d'ye think?"

"Damn Toon Dirt . . . "

Jimmy gave us his version of the phrase. This sounded like an accurate replication of the gatekeeper's diatribe but I still could not follow nor pretend to understand.

"Here, I'll tell ye it again, bit slower, write it doon an' get Leochel Cushnie tae translate."

"Leochel Cushnie" was Jimmy's pet name for my girlfriend. In his working life travelling across the Mearns, Deeside and Donside, Jimmy had picked up a fair understanding of the different dialects that are generally described as Doric. My girlfriend had grown up at Leochel Cushnie near Alford, where you are considered bilingual if you can speak English as well as the local tongue. Jimmy and my girlfriend would have great fun swapping words and phrases and comparing notes on their origin and meaning and I was often enthralled in the process. To my view, Doric in all its forms is a glorious spoken language but it does not look nearly as colourful nor as descriptive in print. My version of the gatekeeper's catchphrase read as follows:

"Damn toon dirt. It's nae fit they tak it's fit they connach and blad an the baists winna ait."

Following a consultation with my girlfriend and a confirmation of her interpretation by Jimmy I tried to translate the phrase back into English in a way that one of the modern environmentalists

49

might utter and the best I could come up with could be written as;

"Infernal Urbanites! They are not satisfied with merely exploiting the countryside and reaping what they have not sown, they wreak wanton damage on the fragile ecology and interfere with the digestive balance of the livestock which, as a consequence, fail to thrive."

Which one do you prefer?

# 4. The Influx

Although the successes achieved by Amoco with "Montrose" and BP with "Forties" were not broadcast to the Aberdeen populace or even the Great British Public the inevitable "Chinese Whispers" had reached the Boardrooms of several other major oil companies envious of the prospect of discovering oil in a relatively stable part of the world. I remember my own view as being typical of most of the locals in that this unexpected and unprecedented flurry of activity, welcome as it was, would prove to be a flash in the pan. My sceptical side tended to make me believe some of the articles from "The Observer," the "Morning Star," and others, which suspected that the notoriously devious and scheming Oil Majors were drumming up North Sea and other prospects like Alaska as a foil to the threats of Arab Nationalists like Libya's Muanmar Gaddafi and demonstrate that they had sufficient alternative resources in politically safe areas not to worry about paying more for Middle East supplies or losing out altogether.

On my way back from my regular Sunday night jaunt to the Marcliffe Hotel for a couple of pints and a listen to Hedgehog Pie's able renditions of Fairport Convention's and Lindisfarne's brand of Folk Rock, I stopped off at the Ashvale (having skipped the Stovies and Late Licence option) and bumped into Wally Gumm, the Workshop Foreman at Schlumberger. Wally had come to Aberdeen from Great Yarmouth and his native Norfolk burr had a mid-Atlantic tinge to it. I had encountered a few "Yarmouth Yanks" who, by their exposure to the fairly sizeable expatriate community in their region, had assimilated enough of the American drawl to give them an accent somewhere between the Singing Postman and the Singing Cowboy, but Wally had actually spent a fair bit of time working in Canada so his hybrid dialect was pleasantly acceptable.

"How ya doin' Wally? I see you've managed to track down the best chip shop in Aberdeen. Is that not the best fish supper you've ever had?"

We were proud of our chip shops in Aberdeen. The area was generally depressed with a declining economy, poor housing stock and dismal employment projections. Even our beloved football team, "The Dons," which had flattered to deceive by winning the Scottish Cup in 1970, was on the slide, losing its best players, Joe Harper (to Everton) Martin Buchan (to Manchester United) and its Manager, the talismanic Eddie Turnbull, to Hibernian. Everyone I knew was unstintingly loyal and respectful of our prime source of takeaway food, the "Chipper," and in the league table of outlets it was generally agreed that "The Ashvale" (immortalised in a "Scotland the What" song) was the Number One. I was chastened, therefore, by Wally's blunt response.

"I'm sorry, young John, but that probably is the worst fish supper I've ever come across."

He went on to demonstrate how unacceptable it was by crumbling between his thumb and forefinger the overcooked batter, exposing the dried-out brown-stained flakes of what could be presumed to be haddock but resembled shoe leather in texture. He gave me a piece to sample and I have to admit that I had tasted better in my time but, in common with the rest of my home town, I would not dream of criticising or complaining about any product from our favourite chipper. That would be tantamount to doubting Joe Harper's goal scoring ability or blaspheming in church, not that I or anyone I knew went to church but I hope you get my drift. Wally was unremitting in his tirade and returned to the counter. He was firm and assertive but not ranting.

"'Ere, I'm not 'avin' that."

"Fit's yer problem? Is yer fish nae big enough?" The shop assistant looked bemused.

Moans about quantities served and prices charged were fairly common exchanges and accepted as popular banter but nobody had ever dared to return an offering complaining about the culinary quality, especially a haddock. Aberdeen was Scotland's premier fishing port. Fish was plentiful and relatively cheap so there was no reason to offer second-rate produce. The Ashvale enjoyed their reputation as the premier chipper and even added twopence or threepence to the price of a supper as a mark of its prestige.

"I ain't in the Fish 'n Chip Shop business but if I was an' I served up somethin' like that in Yarmouth or anywhere else I'd get run outa town."

Wally went on to detail the quality issues that he had explained to me and waited patiently for a response. The young girl shop assistant was too nonplussed to offer any comment and merely shrugged before turning to the Fish Frier for suggestions. With his back turned, his head down and busy hands shifting heaps of new sizzling chips from the hot vat to the drainer, the frier mumbled something indecipherable to anyone on the customer side of the counter.

"A' right, ye can hae anither ane, bit ye'll hiv tae wait." The young girl grumbled with no hint of embarrassment and turned to the next punter in the rapidly growing queue. "White Puddin' Supper? Salt 'n vinegar? One an' elevenpence."

I had ordered and been served with my Red Pudding and Pineapple Fritter (no epicure, me) and was tucking into my chips on my way home but felt I should keep Wally company as he waited patiently for his replacement Haddock Supper. As we leaned against the wall at the back of the queue we chatted generally about working in Regent Road, (Wally had worked in worse places) living in Aberdeen (not as cold as Canada) and got on to debating the future prospects of the region. I voiced my cynical opinion that the oil companies were playing a game of Bluff with the Arabs. Once again I was surprised by Wally's view on the subject.

"Don't you believe it! I ain't allowed to tell you who's got what or where it is but, take my word for it, there's a bunch of new oil and gas fields out there. I've seen the logs, the same ones that them bigwigs in London and Houston have on their desks. That's why they're all scouring the world looking for bigger rigs. Within a year or two this place'll be full of Yanks 'n Frogs 'n all sorts. You won't know what's hit ya! But I tell ya, this place is gonna have to buck up its ideas, startin' with the fish 'n chip shops!"

At that, Wally heard the cry that his fish was ready. He approached the counter and was handed his replacement supper without any apology or explanation. Picking up the steaming parcel, smiling graciously, thanking the girl for her patience and looking for some sort of reciprocal response he received only the standard sullen glare, the Aberdeen Shop Assistant's equivalent of "The Evil Eye." You can still get the same look today; it must be a heritable trait. If you want an example, I would suggest you try approaching a particularly fat quine and asking her for the name of her dietician or an exceptionally ugly one and enquiring after her beautician's number.

Wally turned to me, shrugged and strolled off to his parked car, waving his farewell and giving me a knowing smile. As events were to unfold he was proven correct on both counts. The Ashvale faded from its premier position and closed within a few years to be replaced by a succession of Chinese and Indian Takeaways before being resurrected (with bucked up ideas) around the corner in Great Western Road to even greater acclaim and prosperity. More significantly Wally's predicted "Influx" was much quicker and grander than either of us would have or could have anticipated.

Sorting out the mail was not one of my duties at The Service Company but I had a certain curiosity in checking through the more exotic packages, especially the light blue airmail envelopes with their colourful foreign stamps. Pat, Rosemary, Sheila or Chrissie could sift through the boring buff brown stuff with the invoices, statements and remittance advices. They contained only uninspiring information on money spent or money earned.

That did not hold any attraction to any of my senses or ambitions. My wanderlust was taken by the surge of mail arriving from Canada, USA, France, Italy, Netherlands and New Zealand, all addressed to the strange sounding names of people due to arrive with the incoming outfits: Geoservices, Diamant Boart, American

Coldset Corporation and Sedco that would fill the hastily prepared offices at Regent Road.

These were real "Cowboy" names and I painted mental pictures to put figurative brush heads on these handles. "Elmer J. Adkins – Rig Manager" conjured up the image of the solid citizen type in the mould of Gary Cooper as the Sheriff in *High Noon*. "Virgil L. Jeter – Materials Supervisor," would be his able but silent Deputy. And, do you know, that is just about exactly how they turned out to be.

As Wally Gumm had told me, the oil companies had been scouring the globe for suitable rigs to fulfil their ambitious drilling programmes. With projected water depths exceeding 400 feet the jack-up units that were common in the shallower seas off East Anglia and Holland simply could not be used in the Northern Sector and with Force 10 Storm Winds forming eighty foot waves, the compact Drillships that coped admirably in the Gulf of Mexico and West Africa were viable only during the relative calm of our Summer.

The comparatively new heavy-duty semi-submersible units, such as the *Staflo, Neptune 7,* and *Sea Quest,* had been proven to cope with the elements and year-round conditions. These rigs were termed "semi-submersible" as they were capable of floating on a ballast controlled combination of pontoons, sponsons, columns and braces to be towed to the drilling site, where they could be partially submerged to sit on the sea bed or, if the water depth exceeded the workable height of the columns, to float and be held on station by heavy anchors and chain or cable.

In practice these semi-submersibles completed relatively few wells while sitting "on bottom." That remained the domain of the Jack-Up rigs. It was while floating on the surface in water depths of 400—600 feet and more that these larger units showed their particular capability in withstanding severe weather and extreme ocean waves and currents. I am not a physicist or a Naval Architect but have met enough suitably qualified engineers who informed me that the structures displaying the optimum resistance to external pressure are, top of the list, a sphere (try breaking a golf ball,) then a triangle (how about biting a Toblerone,) and then a square or rectangle (that's why things are packed in boxes.) The special configuration of the semi-submersible rigs allowed them to remain floating, keep station and perform deep drilling operations in the worst imaginable ocean conditions. They were not designed to be beautiful.

*Staflo* was rectangular in form with buoyant pontoons supporting cylindrical columns, which in turn supported the deck and drilling rig. It was held on station by Danforth anchors attached to cables of two and a half inch reinforced steel wire rope on powerful windlasses and, since its construction on Teesside in 1965, had performed capably on station; however it had encountered major problems under tow as its great bulk and peculiar configuration militated against maneouevrability.

*Neptune 7* was one of the first "Pentagone" rigs with five pontoons and columns in typically eccentric French layout (The French always try to design things differently) and although it had formidable integral strength it, too, proved awkward in towing and mooring operations and had problems with deckload limitations. Anti-French bias among the American and English decision makers on the Boards of all the leading major oil companies (apart from Total, Fina and Elf, naturally) led to the proliferation of rumours about unreliability and maintenance problems with some of the esoteric equipment built into the Pentagone units and made them difficult to sell.

*Sea Quest* was a triangular semi-submersible of the 135 Series designed for SEDCO by Earl & Wright of San Francisco and built at Harland & Wolff in Belfast, Northern Ireland. The 135 series had an enviable reputation for build quality and was marginally easier in towing and mooring but also suffered from limited deckload capacity. Partly in the interests of appeasing the jingoistic prejudices of the BP engineers involved in the design and construction along with the protectionist policies of its lords and masters (BP was part owned by the UK Government until 1986) some of the main components such as the Paxman Diesel engines and Ransome cranes were of British manufacture and *Sea Quest* suffered reliability problems but, as BP both owned and operated this rig all gripes and groans were contained within their own happy household.

The *SEDCO 135F* was the newest addition to the 135 Fleet. Built in Vancouver in 1967 it had completed a "shake down" well off Western Canada before being towed to the South Pacific for a two and a half year drilling programme with Shell New Zealand. *SEDCO 135F* had performed in a perfectly acceptable manner but Shell had not achieved the commercial results it had hoped for and, as a consequence, the rig was released from contract. In a seller's market, Shell and SEDCO had little difficulty in finding a new charterer, with Amoco snapping up the option, paying a reputed $2 Million Mobilisation Fee, to take it to the North Sea for a then unheard of rate of $20,000 per day. It had an edge on the *Sea Quest* (which started and ended its life as the *SEDCO 135C*) in that it used three-inch chain rather than wire rope anchor cable, giving it superior mooring properties, and it enjoyed better reliability with its US made EMD engines and Manitowoc and Clyde Cranes.

I knew little or nothing about rigs and their equipment in April 1971 but was eager to come face to face with these auspicious characters with the cowboy names. To my mild initial disappointment but eventual pleasure the first SEDCO visitors were not Elmer and Virgil but Bill Hogg and Pat Devery. They arrived one typically cold and grey Tuesday morning in April. Bill was an affable New Zealander with a shock of fair hair slicked back in a quiff and black rimmed glasses that gave him some resemblance to a chunkier version of Michael Caine. Pat was also a Kiwi with a round face, round features and a permanent chuckle.

As we swapped notes over a cup of tea and a "Rowie," I learned that Bill was a Driller, obviously a key job. In common with most of his colleagues Bill had come from an agricultural background and had worked his way up from the floor to his position of prominence. I had a little difficulty in picking up on Pat's dialect. I know that the

Scots do not waste too much effort on pronouncing vowels but Kiwis seem to dispense altogether with the need to separate consonants. When I enquired about his background I discovered that he had a nautical training and that his skills were employed on the marine side of rig operations where his job title was "Wytchstennor". Not interpreting fully and ever curious I asked him to elaborate on what all was related to this obviously important role.

As Pat rattled on about valves and pumps and tanks and ballast and other esoteric stuff I picked up that he must be the Captain or Barge Master, as I had heard it described on UK rigs, but he corrected me, telling me that he was the assistant to the Barge Engineer (as Americans termed the position). I am pretty hopeless on technical matters and find difficulty with understanding abstract descriptions of mechanical operations but I usually indulge the technophiles, especially those as enthusiastic as Pat Devery, by nodding and "Uh-huh"-ing until they have finished their incomprehensible babblings. I was intrigued by the description of his duties but still puzzled by the title I asked if he would write it out for me which he duly did on the back of a rowie bag.

"Ah! WATCHSTANDER," I enunciated carefully. "So you're paid to stand and watch?"

"Yeah, that's about right!" Pat concurred.

Pat and Bill shared the joke and went on to say that life offshore was not all hectic and there could be a fair amount of time spent waiting for things to happen. There would be moments of spectacular activity but one needed to be prepared for extended periods of extreme boredom in preparation for "The Big Day" which was the day of the crew change when a person could go ashore and enjoy the fruits of their labours.

Rig hands worked on a 14/7 basis with fourteen days on board followed by seven ashore. Wages were good in comparison with shore-based workers and working conditions on the rig were generally considered as very acceptable with good food and clean quarters. Rapid promotion to the prestigious position of Driller or Barge Engineer was available to those prepared to learn and apply themselves. All this sounded quite attractive and I was eager to learn more. Bill and Pat explained that they were the "Advance Party" and that would be several more of their colleagues arriving within the next few days after their scheduled crew change and I would have the chance to meet Larry Harter, George Cawsey, Carl Elter and others.

They would all be looking for houses, schools, cars and household appliances and I was starting to appreciate what Wally Gumm had meant when he spoke of an influx. Of primary importance, however, as the clock headed toward Midday, was the need to track down a suitable bar. New Zealanders have an approach to drinking similar to the Scots, formed by similar backgrounds where an almost identical opening and closing regime had been imposed by Calvinistic lawmakers, and Bill and Pat had just hit shore after a forty-five day tow from Cape Town Gran Canaria.

Aberdeen was not at all well served by way of restaurants and watering holes in 1971 and I was spluttering some sort of apology for our lack of fine wining and dining compared, say, with London or Paris, or any of the exotic spots that high rolling oilmen might have enjoyed. To my knowledge there were only about three places where a gourmet could indulge in anything resembling an *a la carte menu* with a selection of wines. Of the hundred or so licensed establishments in the City about ninety were "spit 'n sawdust" affairs. The remainder were mainly pathetic attempts at the Cocktail Lounge concept. In between there was a range of affordable cafes and luncheonettes, which barely matched up even to the Ashvale.

"No worries, John, all we're looking for is a decent pub with good beer, we can get some tucker back at the hotel later. Where d'ya recommend?"

My circle of friends and family had fairly well defined preferences when it came to visiting drinking establishments. Most of the family would support their "Local" i.e. the pub closest to home (unless they had been "barred" previously.) My football team-mates at Shamrock usually gravitated to the pub nearest to wherever we had been playing or training. We trained on Thursdays at St.Katherine's Club, from seven to nine, and before ten o'clock closing managed to down a couple at Murdo's little hideaway in West North Street. If our game was at Inverdee, then it would be followed by a call at the Brig O' Dee Bar. Some of our key players often made their first call to the bar before kick-off but that's a different story.

If we played at Hazlehead or Aulton, where no suitable bars were available, we would take the bus back into town and drop by the Club Bar in Market Street, where they served the best pies, or The Moorings on Trinity Quay, where they had the best stocked Jukebox. When in the company of our girlfriends or wives we would seek out slightly more sophisticated venues with comfier seats, muted music and cocktail sticks (a Sweet Martini was deemed undrinkable without at least three Maraschino Cherries) and had moved on from The Silver Slipper which had dated formica tables, plywood chairs, loud music and no ice cubes to the recently refurbished Star & Garter boasting dimpled padded vinyl banquettes, carpets, flock wallpaper and a gilt framed poster print of "Cherry Ripe" behind the bar. The epitome of "Posh."

As I delivered a summary of my prevailing views on Aberdeen's hostelries Bill and Pat checked their watches and suggested that they do their own research, but asked for my idea of the best starting point. As it was a Tuesday and The Moorings (which would have been my first choice as an evening venue) would have been empty I plumped for the Star & Garter, ordered them a TODA Taxi and waved them off.

When I met them again later in the week they thanked me for the advice and told me that they had done a tour of most of the pubs around the area from their base in the Imperial Hotel in Exchange Street, had sampled the delicious meat pies at the Club, enjoyed the lively atmosphere and music of The Moorings but went for The Star & Garter as their first choice and had arranged to make that their meeting point when their mates arrived from Gran Canaria.

From that day on and for about the next fifteen years the "Starry" would become a focal point in the shorebase activities of itinerant oilmen and, in contrast to the normal pub exchanges on weather and football, it was interesting to witness groups of roustabouts, roughnecks, derrickmen, drillers (and wannabe drillers) debating the merits and demerits of various tongs, elevators, slips and bushings that they used in the performance of their mysterious activities. By 1973 it was reckoned there were more wells drilled in the "Starry" than in the whole of the North Sea.

When the inevitable shortage of crew-members arose during the "Boom Years" of 1973 -1975 and not enough roughnecks could be found to form a drilling crew it was a common joke in SEDCO's Personnel Department to send a Taxi and a wad of fivers to the Star & Garter. For the first time to my knowledge my personal recommendation had led to significant social and commercial success and although Bill Hogg and Pat Devery and the rest of the *SEDCO 135F* crew voiced their appreciation to me, I never had as much as a free pint from Bill Sked (The Owner) who enjoyed the considerable pleasure and profit from the patronage of the newcomers.

My increasing exposure to this new industry naturally made me want to share the exciting ideas and opportunities with family and friends. The original scepticism in my mind had been assuaged and was gradually being replaced with genuine enthusiasm and, for once, optimism. My own wages had been increased from £12 to £22 per week and with regular overtime my income was now on a par with most of my contemporaries but, patently, a long way off the money that those boys going offshore could earn.

Promotion prospects based on personal performance rather than the nepotism that was prevalent in British industry and the potential for international travel rather than a dead end job in dingy Aberdeen were particularly attractive options to my view but these were not readily shared even by those of my associates that I considered to be open minded and ambitious. Job security was a key issue, as nobody could be sure that this fledgling industry would last, far less predict the kind of monster that would arise to dominate the economy and lifestyle of our beloved North East of Scotland.

Hiring and firing practices as reported in the Media and exaggerated by hearsay were anathema to most of my left-leaning associates (which comprised most of my working class family, football friends and ex-University colleagues.)

Virtually everybody I knew was a Socialist of some hue from blush pink to fiery red. The dangers of helicopter and ship travel on treacherous seas to notoriously unsafe vessels were not immediately off-putting but, as stories filtered down from the incomers who had been inured to the extremes of wind and weather and from the few locals who had dared to venture out to the North Sea, they added to the growing doubts as to the attractiveness of a "job on the rigs." Not many takers, early doors.

The day in April 1971, when Elmer Adkins and Virgil Jeter arrived in Aberdeen, was very much a key moment not only for them, as they made preparations for the arrival in the North Sea from halfway around the world of their much vaunted drilling rig, but also for the Service Company as we prepared to entertain, accommodate and service one of the most important and biggest value contracts in Aberdeen's history.

As I had only had about six months' of very minor exposure to any business in general and this "Oil" business in particular, I think I can be excused for my naïve underestimation of the scale of the project. Jim Simpson was much better informed and aware of the risks and benefits involved. That is why he had ordered the stripping out of the old mill machinery and the hasty preparation of offices at Regent Road and that is why he was there in person to meet and greet the newcomers from SEDCO.

Jim had been involved in earlier meetings between Mitch Watt and his senior officers at AMOCO and Walter Etherington, Sedco's Vice Pesident in London, as they negotiated terms and conditions on this multi-million dollar contract to bring the *SEDCO 135F* from New Zealand and, although comfortable on a social level with these affable wheeler dealers, he was probably out of his depth on any commercial basis. Jim's management style was very much "hands off," as, from the founding of ASC in 1967, most of the activity had been of a physical nature (Dubs) and, not being a very technical chap, he had delegated all of that to the more than capable Jimmy Gallan.

It was untypical to see much of Jim Simpson in his office at Regent Road unless there were VIP's in attendance, so when he rolled up that April morning with Elmer and Virgil in tow we figured that these must be "Big Wheels" and of course, as Rig manager and Material Supervisor of the *135F*, they were, but, meeting them in person, the first impression that I got was how pleasant and natural they were. This impression endured as I got to know them both fairly well over the following three or four years. There was no pomp or pretensions of power, just a keen focus on the job in hand and a genuine interest in the people paid to perform that job. Popularist pragmatism.

Elmer, particularly, had a calm, avuncular presence and a ready reassuring smile. He always displayed a keen interest in a person's feelings as well as his function. He gave us an early lesson in the art of man-management and it was obvious from the comments of the rig hands, who had arrived earlier, that he had natural charisma and had earned their respect and loyalty by setting and recognising good standards of behaviour and performance.

Elmer was no "soft touch" however, and I was present on a few occasions to witness his particularly honest, effective but inoffensive delivery of a well-earned rebuke or dismissal if someone fell short of those standards. The message that we received from their customers, (those hard bitten, avaricious, grasping, megalomaniac oil companies) was that Elmer's approach worked and that he and others like him in the SEDCO organisation had developed the best "Iron" (Rig Equipment) and the highest rated "Hands" (Drilling Crews.) Who was I to argue?

Virgil, too, in his tall. angular frame and chiselled features, had an assured bearing. He followed Elmer's example and fitted in well with the ethos but did not exhibit the same levels of patience and forbearance. He had a bit of a short fuse which some attributed to his red hair, but both were generally well controlled, his hair brushed back carefully and his occasional lapses in decorum relieved by a puff on a Peter Stuyvesant.

During our very early discussions on setting up their new offices Elmer graciously thanked us for our hard work in getting the place ready while Virgil made a list of their requirements by way of desks, chairs, phones and other paraphernalia. Out of idle curiosity I asked them when the rest of their office entourage would be arriving. I was drawing comparisons with Shell's *Staflo* organisation in Market Street where they had a headcount of forty-four (and rising) and BP's relatively slim *Sea Quest* operation in Bridge Street where they managed to get by with only about sixteen.

So I had difficulty comprehending Elmer's response, when he said that they would be running their rig as they had done everywhere else in the world, with just the two of them plus an accountant, Brian Tobin, who was due to arrive from New Plymouth, a couple of secretaries and two warehousemen, a paltry total of seven. In order to satisfy my enquiring mind I shot them a line of questions to determine who would look after each of the departments that I knew Shell had assigned to the key functions of running their *Staflo* rig.

"Won't you have a drilling team? Jock Munro has about four experts on drilling in the Shell office."

"We got all the guys we need on the rig to look after drilling. I'm here in the office in case the client wants to ask a question."

"How about the Barge Department? Ries van Dijk must have another three Captains and towing experts to help him."

"Roy and the boys keep the rig floatin' and moored. They don't need no help from here in town."

"And Purchasing? Cliff Kitchin's got five or six helping him buy the parts."

"We just buy enough to keep it turnin' to the right. An' we never overpay!"

"How about Material Control? Looking after your movable assets, There's about four of them over at Market Street."

"Virgil has a handle on everything we own."

"Ah, how about the warehouse and yard? Shell must have a dozen hands at Torry Dock."

"We reckon those two hands, Hugh and Bruce, that you fixed us up with ought to be able to cope with our stock and supplies."

"Personnel? Stan Brands must have about six helpers to handle that."

"When it comes to people, Logan and Larry push the tools and make sure everybody is safe and happy in their job. Brian Tobin and one of the girls will make sure they're paid."

"Well, I guess I can see how you won't need the six extra people that Shell have for office services."

"That's right, the less people you have, the less you need. We can fix our own coffee."

"Oh, how about Transport? Shell's got four guys handling boats, choppers, and trucks."

"That's y'all's job! That's what we hired you for, right?"

Virgil's comment about my new responsibilities was delivered in his normal friendly way but I could tell from Elmer's supportive nod of assent that he was not joking. For the first time (but definitely not the last) in my subsequent twenty-plus year association with SEDCO I was being dumped in the Deep End. Jim Simpson had only partially prepared me for this, by telling me that I would be doing SEDCO's "Customs," which I imagined would be on a par with the two easily paced mornings that I did at Shell filling in forms and photocopying manifests. In truth Jim had oversold the capabilities of our service company and I grew to learn that his over-confidence was eroding the credibility of his clients as well as his backers.

Although I was confident that I could cope with the Customs paperwork I was a bit wary on the logistics as The Service Company had no suitable trucks, cranes or yard space to handle the Marine Riser, Drillpipe and other tubulars that come along with every mobile rig unit. Apart from all of that I still did not have a driving licence.

It proved to be a very steep learning curve but, in spite of several pitfalls, we got through it in very good humour and established a very enjoyable working relationship. My new duties meant that I was in regular contact with Virgil and became almost a member of their staff; so much so that they would involve me in their recruiting activities. I knew then, as I know now, that I could never be a successful Personnel Officer (I'm too honest for a start) but I relished the idea of finding suitable applicants for vacant positions.

None of my friends had asked me to find them a job. Many would relent in later years but in 1971 most were still too dubious. Virgil needed two Warehousemen to fix up and run the Shorebase Stores Function. We fixed him up with Hugh Webster (from the Gordon Graham store which was due to close) and Bruce Rothnie. They settled in well and, in spite of a little early friction, both went on to enjoy successful careers in the industry.

Elmer said he would need to find up to forty new recruits to fill the positions from Roustabout up to Assistant Driller to replace the New Zealanders and Australians for whom they could not obtain work permits. As hard as I tried and as much as I wanted to help my old and new friends alike, I could find no suitable candidates. SEDCO advertised in local and national newspapers but were having mixed success. The rest of the nation seemed to share Aberdeen's lethargy and scepticism about the validity of these opportunities in a new industry and a testing environment.

As I strolled down the cobbled lane into Regent Road one early morning in May I passed the entrance to the SEDCO/AMOCO suite to see, sitting on the stairs up to the offices, half a dozen young guys, two of whom I thought I recognised but did not know too well. The first one I spotted was Jeff Nicol, a Panel Beater at Charlic Alexander Transport and part-time Bouncer.

Here is an interesting sociologal observation. In his role as bouncer at The Moorings Jeff could be a snarling, unremitting thug, even to a mild mannered, unassuming soul such as myself; however, sitting on someone else's doorstep, which he presumed to be mine, hoping for an entry, he suddenly exuded charm and courtesy.

The other was John Douglas, who had previously worked at Schlumberger but had given up in favour of more stable employment back onshore They had heard through the grapevine that SEDCO were hiring that day and, as they were both committed to working offshore, they had come along early to make sure of their place in the queue.

Along with them (and three others whom I did not know) was Michael Inglis, a welder from Hall Russell, our local shipyard.

We chatted a bit. Jeff was fed up with the poor rates and lack of prospects at Charlie Alexander and wanted to give the rig business a try. John had regretted giving up but on his previous job could not get his place back at Schlumberger and wanted back offshore as soon as possible. Michael was bored with the yards and fearful that he would be laid off as soon as the next ship was finished.

There is a happy end to this tale as all six of the lads on the step were hired on that day and went on to achieve some of the success that they sought. I don't know anything about the three strangers but Jeff went on to climb the promotion ladder and became a Rig Superintendent offshore Brazil. John reached the same heights and the last I heard he was in South Africa. The only story I heard about Mike the Welder may be apocryphal but it is so good, in explaining the concept of the learning and adapting to the brave new world, that it bears repeating:

"It may have been the first or second well drilled by the *135F* (the first was over very quickly as the wellbore entered a pocket of surface gas which has killer potential for a floating rig and had to be abandoned) and a very green crew was being shown through its paces by the experienced but slightly tetchy supervisors.

"Everybody was being ultra cautious as we were at a critical part of the operation, when the thirty-inch conductor pipe had to be fed through the rotary table, the substructure and the moonpool before being landed on the wellhead. Each thirty-inch conductor is a forty-foot long steel cylindrical tube, weighing about six tons and fitted with one-inch padeyes to help with lifting while in horizontal mode. Before insertion into the wellbore the conductor has to be held on a "spider" (frame) in the moonpool while these padeyes are removed.

"It was night, it was dark and as the weather was deteriorating, there was increasing urgency to finish the task as soon as practicable. In charge of the operation was Tourpusher (nightshift Rig Superintendent) Gerald Kalmbach, a Canadian with a thick German accent, a good deal of experience, redoubtable technical capability and a fairly fiery temper. As the conductor was being lowered gingerly on to the spider deck Gerald barked at Mike Inglis, the welder.

'Velder, get me a torch!'

Mike hastened off to his workshop nearby in the moonpool eager to show a willing attitude.

'There ye are, Boss.'

Mike was back in seconds handing the torch carefully to to an increasingly anxious Kalmbach.

'Mother \*\*\*\*\*\*! Zat's a flashlight, sonuvabitch! Vot I need is a torch, a burner. Go get me a goddam "Gas Axe!'

Highly embarrassed but grasping the point and the urgency, Mike returned to his workshop and wheeled out the Oxy-Acetylene burning gear."

Here endeth the first lesson in oilfield linguistics.

# 5. All in a Day's Work

In the ultra-competitive climate of modern Capitalism it is customarily assumed that for a private business the greatest threats to success and prosperity come from those rivals battling for their perceived advantage in the market. One might also expect that, in the notoriously secretive, capital intensive, high technology world of international offshore oil exploration, there would be scant evidence of co-operation and collaboration between competing companies. This is not what I have to report from my experiences in the late summer of 1971.

While we struggled in the formative years of North Sea oil exploration to carve Aberdeen Service Company's niche as a warehousing agent, our only real competition in Aberdeen was the longer established and better-equipped firm of Barrack Transport. They had similarly dilapidated premises and equally worn out trucks but had the edge in that they owned more of each. Activity was sporadic with long idle spells separated by short periods of hyper-activity and it was inevitable that our limited resources would be stretched at times. The surprising thing, at least to me, as a novice in the wicked world of warehousing and transport, was that we would help each other willingly and quite regularly. Barrack would hire our bulker if theirs had broken down. We would hire their articulated lorries if we had to shift loads that were too long for our own trucks.

As the pace of exploration increased and oil companies began to look for suitable sites for storing and handling the larger, heavier items like wellheads and casing pipe, they naturally turned to their existing service providers to find the solution. Our boss, Jim Simpson, ever eager to satisfy the customers needs, had been aware of the forthcoming demands but had been pleading in vain with the local council and Aberdeen Harbour Board to obtain property leases and, for once, he failed to keep the customer satisfied. In consequence our clients were forced to hold their stocks in East Anglia or Teesside and suffer the punitive costs and time delays associated with the long haul of shipping by supply boat to the new northern fields.

Eventually, after much pleading, Jim Simpson went out on a limb and promised to find yardspace and our client, Conoco, who were in line to be the next operator of the *Sedco 135F* rig, arranged to have their first order of wellhead equipment delivered direct to Aberdeen. Only a few days before it all was due to arrive, we still had not found any appropriate sites and we were all suffering a collective anxiety that imposed some stress on the hitherto symbiotic relationship. By good fortune, or good planning, our rivals, Barrack had acquired a property at Abbotswell with a reasonably flat area at the rear, which was deemed fit for pipe storage. They had also purchased a new thirty-ton crane and, while touting its availability and hearing of our plight, offered us a package deal. Had they been ruthless privateers they might have considered stealing a march on the opposition and taken their offer direct to our clients, but the overwhelming spirit at the time was of co-operation rather than competition. We accepted their offer and made arrangements for handling the incoming hardware.

Again, this was done in an atmosphere of mutual help and without any hint of hindrance. In laying out the pipe racks at the Abbotswell yard, our Gaffer, Jimmy Gallan, would lend a hand if Donald, the Barrack crane driver needed help with clearing a trench or positioning a railway sleeper. Donald, or any of the Barrack lads, would equally oblige with tying ropes on an Asco lorry or any other task that required collaboration.

I surmise this was a way of working carried over from the farms where these lads grew up. Demarcation and restrictive practices had not yet entered the vocabulary of the Doric workforce.

The first load to arrive at the Abbotswell Yard was a consignment of twenty-inch Casing Pipe. Each pipe was forty foot long and two tons in weight and, as none of us had any previous experience in

70

handling this equipment, we proceeded slowly and carefully with the offloading. Donald made sure his crane was firmly planted as Jimmy marshalled the incoming trucks and kept an eagle eye on his helpers as they familiarised themselves with the operation.

Bill Byatt, the Conoco Materials Supervisor, had provided the proper lifting slings along with a set of "Pipe Brothers" (hooks specially designed for safe handling of casing) and handed me the Rabone Chesterman tape, along with the tally book for measuring the lengths of pipe and recording them as they were being stowed.

A Rabone Chesterman! That was the kind of tape that some of my friends who were ploughing their furrow as Quantity Surveyors or Town Planners would have to guard with their lives during their working day. They were obviously top notch pieces of kit, with wax coated linen tape enclosed in an almond coloured leather case, polished brass fittings and a feel of quality associated with Fortnum & Mason hampers and Purdy shotguns. They cost about £27 each for the standard Imperial tape in feet and inches and slightly more for the dual gauge in Metric thingummies; but this was a special tape calibrated in "Tenths of a Foot," manufactured specifically for the oil industry. Bill did explain the origins of this eccentricity of measurement but I forget the details, I think it was something to do with the inability of Americans to cope with long division by twelve. Anyway, this tape was split new and cost £42 and I was in charge of it. Some business this oil game!

Back to the work in progress; all eyes were carefully focussed on the hooks as Donald slewed the jib and they arced through the air in preparation for the first lift. With the "brothers" firmly secured, he eased the hydraulic controls until the slings tightened and the crane hoisted the pipe slowly skywards.

"Float 'em ower, Donald!" was Jimmy Gallan's careful exhortation as he watched the casing being guided toward the rack where it landed gently on the prepared bed of sleepers. The same keen attention was paid to each length of pipe until the first load had been completed and the next truck rolled in. Before lunchtime we had handled five loads and considered this a job well done.

Bill and I had plenty time to run the tape and tally the lengths in complete safety. I took great care to ensure there were no kinks in the Rabone Chesterman.

As we paused for the next load a young lad emerged from the office and approached us eagerly. It was Hamish Barrack, the son of the owner, with urgent new orders.

"Donald, we've another job on for two o'clock. You'll need to go back to Canal Road and take the old crane over to Brig o Don."

"Ay, Hamish, but we'll need tae feenish this ane first. We've anither five load yet."

"Dinna worry aboot that. I can handle it myself"

"But ye hinna driven this thing yet, Hamish. Are ye sure?"

"Oh aye, I had a shottie of the demonstrator afore we bought it. It's a hydraulics. Caker."

With Hamish's reassurance that all was in order, Donald calmly dismounted and headed back to Barrack's HQ at Canal Road, leaving the boss's son in charge of the new crane. I had not met Hamish before. He was a little younger than myself but displayed all the confidence of a seasoned pro. He climbed into the cabin and started issuing instructions while re-acquainting himself with the controls. The workers looked wary but set to resuming the task in hand.

There was a marked contrast in the motion of the crane jib as Hamish fumbled with the various knobs and levers. Whereas Donald's handling had resulted in slow, steady, almost graceful movements that could be likened to the motion of a baton in the hands of a classical conductor, the crane under Hamish's control lurched and jerked like an axe in the hands of a frenzied assassin. The boys on the truck had to keep their wits about them as the hooks descended in a vicious swirl. They secured the brothers and stood well clear as the pipe was hoisted skyward. The boys on the ground were equally cautious and waited until the pipe was lowered below head height before attempting to guide it into place and release the slings.

Hamish maintained a relentless stream of cheery cajoling

eager to convince all within earshot that there was no element of danger, while he began to master his new toy. To be fair, he was a quick learner but the emphasis was on the "quick" rather than the "learner." He had three truckloads emptied in the time that Donald had taken to complete just two but the telling factor was in the appearance of the finished stacks of pipes. The pile that Donald had assembled could be compared to the formation that you might see in a newly opened pack of cigarettes, with all the tubes neatly interwoven in a symmetrical pattern and perfectly flush at the end. By contrast, Hamish's end result resembled the pile of straws that you would see after a nursery class's enthusiastic game of "Pick-Up-Sticks."

With the first load finished we started to offload the wellhead items that had arrived during the morning. These were awkward pieces built from heavy steel and individually stowed in strong wooden skids packed tightly into closed containers. The intricacy of the arrangement led to a bit of head scratching as Jimmy, Hamish and the gang pondered the best way to handle it.

We had been joined by a representative of the wellheads manufacturer, Cameron Iron Works, in the person of Herb Bourque who looked and sounded like a young John Wayne. Herb was there to ensure that all the required components were accounted for. As an experienced Sub Sea Engineer he had expert knowledge of the equipment. Armed with a detailed packing list, which needed to be tallied against Conoco's purchase order, Herb joined right into the mood of mutual understanding, climbing into the container, eyeballing the kit and giving pointers to Jimmy and the gang as to how to remove the bulky, heavy valuable pieces. Together they worked out a scheme whereby the skids would be dragged by the crane towards the door before being steadied by a pair of forklifts. At that point lifting slings could be applied ready for the crane to hoist and place carefully on the hardcore beds that Jimmy and Donald had prepared.

The first pieces to be offloaded were relatively small crates with green painted semi-circular iron plates. Herb identified them as

Wellhead Hold Down Rings and suggested that the crane would be able to handle them without assistance from the forklifts. Hamish set to the task with his customary zeal and jerked the jib into place. As the boys secured the slings and gave the signal to lift, Hamish whizzed the hook block skyward and slewed the crates into midair.

"There's nae weight in these things at a'! I'll plant them furthest awa' an leave space for the heavier pieces closer tae the crane. Whaddya reckon, Herb?"

"Yeah, buddy, sounds mighty fine to me."

With the severe swinging motion, however, the pressure of the wire rope slings started to crush the wooden crate and we all scattered as we heard the creaking timbers and watched the splinters being strewn about our heads. By now Hamish had the crane jib fully extended and, adding to our concerns for personal safety, the overload alarm started ringing. Hamish reacted reasonably well and released the load. This stopped the alarm but sent the crate crashing with a hefty thump as the wood disintegrated releasing the two wellhead plates to find their own resting place in the soft earth just outside the designated hardcore bed.

"Sorry, boys, I didnae mean tae scare ye. I hope your rings are all right, Herb."

"No sweat, Hamish, them suckers can stand any sort of treatment."

We all gathered around the crushed crate as Herb double-checked for any damage. His calm nod of the head and rueful smile indicated that everything was in order and the boys released the slings in preparation for the second lift. Hamish retained his confident smile but conceded that the more demanding tasks of removing the rest of the cargo would probably be beyond his limited expertise and went to seek help. An early solution was at hand, as Barrack's other regular crane driver, Ernie Mutch, arrived on the scene. Ernie came from Ellon and enjoyed a similar agricultural background to Jimmy Gallan and the others. After exchanging the usual pleasantries and discussing the progress of our morning's work he assumed his responsibilities with a calm grace.

"Aye, Hamish, I doot ye'll nivver mak a cran driver. Ye'll need tae stick tae yer lessons."

Hamish returned to the office citing higher commercial priorities and cheerfully left the mechanical handling project in the hands of the professionals. Ernie, Jimmy and Herb had a further discussion and refined the earlier plan for handling the precious cargo. If Donald's handling of the crane jib was like a conductor then it was akin to a magician's wand in Ernie's hand. It was a wonder to behold his management of the levers and his keen eye on the hook, block and jib as well as watching out for the goods and, most importantly, the men who were helping him. With Jimmy Gallan on one forklift and Jock Begg on the other, we had the entire load discharged licketysplit with no damage to the crates nor any risk to life or limb. After it had all been laid out on the hardcore beds, Herb and Bill double checked the kit and signed off the papers. We were all done before teatime.

An emergency arose when the *Sedco 135F* rig, on its first well for Amoco Norway, drilled through a pocket of surface gas. This was an exceedingly hazardous situation for a semi-submersible rig and, as a result, the wellhead had to be abandoned while the rig was towed to a safer location. A new set of wellhead equipment was available from Great Yarmouth but two or three days of valuable rig time would be lost in the shipping process. The high day-rate was foremost in our clients thinking, as we witnessed another example of co-operation between rivals.

Since they were sharing a contract on the same rig and using identical wellhead equipment it might not seem surprising that someone would make the commonsensical suggestion to swap assets, by mobilising Conoco's kit in Aberdeen ahead of the Amoco set from East Anglia, but we should bear in mind that we are discussing major international oil companies engaged in multi-million dollar operations here. I was not privy to all of the conversations but I understand from reliable sources that it took only a few phone calls, inside a couple of hours, to confirm the swapping arrangement. Everything was concluded on a gentleman's agreement and an exchange of Telex messages. There were no Lear Jet flights to high-level parleys, no gathering of legal eagles with bundles of missives or number crunching accountants with their caveats and, most importantly, no delays and no recriminations. A deal was done before dark.

This set me to thinking that the people running this multi-national business, or at least the exploration side of it, were operating on the same principles as Jimmy Gallan and Ernie Mutch and the boys on the farm, which was to get the job done simply and safely with the minimum of fuss and a careful avoidance of wasted effort and resources; it was starting to become interesting to me.

The very next day we received our instructions to ship out all the kit that we had just moved into the Abbotswell yard. This was delivered with the same level of importance as would be given to an order for a delivery of fifty tons of barytes but, even in the heyday of barytes cutting, no cargo had been turned around this quickly. We were astonished but Barracks were delighted. This meant more hires for their cranes and trucks. We were rewarded only with the ship's agency work, which was extremely interesting but relatively unrewarding financially. My task would be to check off all the items as they arrived at Pocra Quay for loading to the *Smit Lloyd 103*. This was made easier by having a copy of the checklist that Bill and Herb had prepared the day before.

Everything appeared to be going to plan as we watched the final truckload arrive at quayside. All the items had been stowed carefully on the ship's deck with the pipes in neat parallel lines on the foredecks and the heavy wellheads at the aft end to facilitate discharge at the rig. As the dockers anticipated an early finish to their shift I tallied the items on the truck against my checklist. I could not see the Wellhead Hold Down Plates. I retained a mental picture of the green rings that Hamish had dumped unceremoniously in the dirt only the day before. They were not there. They must have been left behind at Abbotswell. Without the aid of radios, and well before the availability of mobile phones, there was no option but to drive across town and fetch the missing items.

I hitched a lift with Elmer Adkins, the Sedco Rig Manager. There was no real reason for Elmer to be there at the quayside. This was the operator's equipment. He was the contractor. No skin off his nose if something was lost and his rig was delayed, at $20K dayrate, but that was not in Elmer's nature. He was like Jimmy and Ernie and the other boys on the farm. If somebody needed help and he was available he would offer to help where he could.

Along the way we picked up Herb Bourque. I had a good idea of what we were looking for and I think Elmer trusted me but, as I came to learn, he was always a "belt and braces" guy and wanted to be sure that we picked the right thing; he knew that Herb knew what to look for. Jock Begg followed in the Ford Transit. We remembered, from Hamish's ham-fisted handling, that the rings weighed less than a ton; the Transit could handle that much and would be quicker through the late afternoon traffic that beset Aberdeen even as far back as 1971.

Arriving at Abbotswell we found the missing pieces, but learned that the crane had gone and the only means of lifting the wellhead plates was Barrack's forklift. Jock appeared in the Transit and reversed it carefully along the road beside the green painted plates, still looking forlorn lying amongst the crumbled pieces of crate in the soft earth where they had been dumped the day before. As the forklift was steered into place we discovered that the earth was too loose to support the weight of the truck and could not get close enough to complete the lift. We all appeared at a loss as to how to recover the stranded pieces. It would take more than an hour to get the crane back. That would lead us into an overtime situation with the dockers, and there was no guarantee that the Harbour Board crane would still be available. This whole project, which had been brilliantly conceived by like minded executives and operatives was foundering.

As we all discussed the situation and mulled over the options and their costs, not least of which involved the downtime of the precious rig, Jock Begg merely shrugged his shoulders, took off his heavy jacket and ambled over to the crumpled heap of valuable cargo.

"Nivver heed, I'll shift it for ye."

"Hey, Jock, be careful, them suckers weigh three hundred pounds each," Herb cautioned.

"Aye, three hunnerwecht, that's aboot the same weight as a stuck ploo, an I've liftit a few o them afore noo."

Without any fuss or strain Jock straddled the stranded plates, grasped them with his bare hands, and lifted them clear of the mud one at a time, carrying them over the soft earth on to the hard metalled road, where he calmly hoisted them on to the forks of the lift-truck, wrapped a wire rope sling around them and proceeded to load the bundle on to the back of the Transit.

He then drove back to the quayside and had them delivered as the dockers were trundling back from their "Smoko." Elmer, Herb and I arrived just in time to witness the pair of green rings being landed on the supply boat. Bill Byatt arrived to check the manifest and despatch the *Smit Lloyd 103*. With customary politeness he expressed his usual appreciation for everyone's co-operation.

"Well, chaps, that was quite a team effort, thank you all."

"Yea, sure, Bill, thanks for the nice words," said Herb. "But this was no team effort, that gorilla did it all hisself."

We all looked at Jock Begg in pride and admiration. Totally unperturbed, he responded in his own inimitable fashion.

"Weel, I suppose that's anither day's work deen."

The spirit of co-operation that we witnessed that day was typical of the age, a credit to the key players and a source of encouragement for the optimists of this earth. Within a very short time afterwards, however, the cynics amongst us would be gratified to observe the decline of this symbiosis and a reversion to a "dog eat dog" culture. During 1972, amid the media ballyhoo that accompanied the announcement of the discoveries of "Forties" and "Brent," we were increasingly confronted by a different kind of newcomer and a different attitude.

Where we had been amused and cheered by the arrival of

the colourful cowboys there was a feeling of unwanted intrusion relating to the increasing preponderance of "suits" arriving in our midst. By this I mean the typically pin-striped suit clad, old school tie wearing, plummy voiced plutocrats representing merchant banks and other investment vehicles who had no knowledge of our business, our region or our people but had obviously been attracted by the tales of enormous earnings that would be made from the North Sea Bonanza.

Now, don't get me wrong. I hold no prejudices based on a person's appearance, their mode of dress or their manner of speech. There were quite a few amongst us who favoured pin-striped suits. Peter Marshall would always put on his blue chalk-striped outfit when visiting customers. There were some who were glad to display an affinity with their place of education. Alex Forbes would regularly and proudly display his fondness for his Alma Mater by donning his Gordonians tie. Plummy voices were rare but, as long as the message was consistent and constructive, the speaker would be well received.

Ron Balls of Amoco had a pronounced form of delivery, which could be derided as la-di-da. In sharing the *Sea Quest* contract, Ron would be in regular contact with his counterpart at BP, the gruff-spoken, jocular Bob Dyer. Bob liked to mock Ron's posh tone and would take delight in calling the Amoco office knowing that Ron would pick up the phone and respond with a businesslike "Balls, Amoco" to which Bob would reply, tersely, "Dyer, 'ere" (evoking the digestive condition) before dissolving into chuckles. Ron would utter a deep sigh before continuing their exchanges. They got on famously.

During 1972 both Asco and Barracks, in their privileged position in the perceived Klondyke, would receive overtures from merchant bankers and the like. I encountered quite a few in the Asco office as they beat a path to Jim Simpson's door. They were markedly different from the explorationists like Mitch Watt, Buster Iversen and Jock Munro. Those guys were interesting and interested at the same time and genuinely approachable. They knew their business and were aware of the importance of working together on a human level to achieve their real aims. In contrast the new wave of visitors appeared ignorant and unapproachable. Invariably, they wore pin-striped suits, ties that I failed to recognise, and spoke in plummy accents, but that is not a value judgment.

Within the camp of unattractive suitors I remember fending off all sorts of hopefuls and hopeless, even some high-ranking officers of reputable UK corporations. We had a general awareness that Asco would require outside assistance in order to achieve its mighty potential and entertained our fantasies by imagining our being sought and bought by some go-ahead multi-national like Brown & Root or MacDermotts or obtaining a capital injection from one of the major banks. I was surprised when a team arrived from Sidlaw Industries. On face value they appeared to be especially unattractive and disinterested and I was surprised when Jim Simpson appeared to greet them warmly and usher them in to his hallowed chamber.

At the same time we heard that Barracks were also being pursued and it was no surprise when we heard of their takeover by a venture capitalist and the formation of a new service company in the guise of Seaforth Maritime. By the end of 1972, Asco had also been acquired by Sidlaw and we had two completely different organisations with new owners and entirely new sets of working arrangements.

The single most important difference that I noticed and the salient point in this tale of co-operation in working life is that we no longer called on each other to help out in a crisis. Asco had been provided with sufficient capital to buy brand new articulated trucks in gleaming dark blue livery. Seaforth had equipped their new acquisition with an impressive fleet of maroon coloured vehicles. On the rare occasion that Seaforth did enquire about hiring an Asco truck we were instructed to quote it at a premium rate of £7.50 rather than the standard £6.00 per hour. We got a similar response when we went looking for a truck. The days of friendly co-operation were over. We were now pitched against each other.

# 6. Forties Makes A Mark

As most of the activity in Regent Road centred around mud handling (Dubs,) it was difficult to appreciate all the other various factors and components of the offshore drilling and exploration industry. We had Schlumberger in their workshop in the south east corner with all their sophisticated gadgetry. Even if any of us had an affinity with complex mechanical and electronic equipment, and we had several good friends including Jim Webster, Ricky Mearns and Lennie Moggach who had made the giant leap from beer bottling and working on wagons with Gordon Graham to the esoteric demands of the world's leading Well Service Contractor to teach us, it would have been a demanding quest to try to learn much about Schlumberger's business as every operation was always cloaked in secrecy.

BP's *Sea Quest* operation was also something of an enigma. They had leased a sizeable section (about 1500 square feet) of warehouse space immediately north of the Schlumberger shop but rarely held any equipment or spares. This was in stark contrast to the *Staflo* operation managed by Shell, which had an office and warehouse complex filling the whole of the former Corporation Tram Shed at 244 Market Street, on the corner of North Esplanade West, with a staff of about forty-four and a vast array of high value rig spares.

The man in charge of the BP warehouse was the dapper Captain Stanislav Adamaszek, a retired Polish Merchant Mariner who had anglicised his name to Stanley Adams. He was the first, but not the last person to suggest that BP Exploration ran their business on tight, economic principles whereas Shell were prone to excessive bureaucracy, over-manning and unnecessary expense.

This view was confirmed on my regular visits to Market Street for the mundane task of filling in Shell's Customs forms. One of my main contacts there was Jim Allison, a well-educated and capable chap, who understood the systems and procedures but was sensitive to any perceived criticism of his cherished employer. Jim explained that much of the Shell bureaucracy and office politics emanated from the necessity to satisfy both the British and Dutch management factions, as well as the interests of their exploration partner, Esso, who were sharing the costs in their highly speculative and expensive joint venture.

Jim applied his natural cynicism in outlining their Personnel Policy. It was generally held that a job at Shell was a job for life. It was conceivable that a member of staff could be fired but to do so, one would have to do something drastic like shooting their boss, in which case Shell would probably have engaged a high priced QC to defend the assailant. Another opinion widely shared within their vast enterprise was that other organisations, BP in particular, enjoyed greater success in their exploration. As Jim Allison put it, pithily:

"Shell couldn't find oil in a garage!"

There were several rumours circulating in the industry during the frenzied efforts in the "Drilling Season" of 1970 that some of the participants had struck oil, "Paydirt" as it was quaintly termed, but in spite of continuous attempts since 1965, Shell still had nothing to reward their considerable investment.

On my way back from Market Street to Regent Road one Thursday lunchtime in November 1970 I was met by an unusually anxious Stanley Adams, who asked in hushed, nervous tones whether he could hire our forklift that afternoon. Stanley had always been exceptionally careful with BP's expenditure and was reluctant to incur the hourly charge of £2.50 unless he had a full workload that would justify the outlay. For single lifts of heavy cargo he would generally prefer to barter some of his valuable photocopies on his Xerox 600 or coffee and biscuits from his well-protected hoard. Now he wanted to hire the Henly Hawk for an entire afternoon! In addition he wanted someone "trustworthy" to help him sort out some precious cargo that was due to arrive that day. I was intrigued and volunteered for the task.

Stanley took me into his office and, continuing in his mysterious undertone, explained in careful detail what had to be done. A covered wagon had been loaded at BP's base in Dundee that morning with a cargo from *Sea Quest* and was to arrive in Aberdeen at 2pm. This wagon was to be driven right up to the door of the BP warehouse where the load of wooden boxes would be offloaded and taken out of the sight of others into the lockable store. A Geologist from BP was to join us; he was going to direct the separation and marking of these boxes. I started to realise the importance of this project when Stanley presented me with a brand new black "Mark-All" felt-tip marker pen (thirty pence each). Thirty pence! That was an hour's wages for me.

At the time I did not understand why the boxes had to be hidden from "prying eyes," but I have concluded in the intervening years that this consignment of boxes contained the core samples from the exploration well that proved to be the most significant oil discovery in the history of North Sea development—Forties.

We can all appreciate the need for secrecy in such a momentous event, and at that time Regent Road was a regular calling point for all manner of explorationists from a range of international oil companies, people like Mitch Watt of Amoco, Buster Iversen of Conoco, Jock Munro from Shell all visiting Jim Simpson in his office (which was within 15 yards of the BP store) to "shoot the breeze," drink some Vintage Port or distinguished Single Malts and discuss plans for future North Sea activity. All of these guys and others from Unocal, Ashland, Sunoco who passed through Regent Road in 1970 were seasoned professionals and would have guessed in an instant what these boxes might contain.

About the same time I recall an occasion when Helen Whyte, PA to the Schlumberger boss, Yves Leroux, stomped into Asco's lean-to office, commandeered one of our telephones and, in a stern tone, ordered us out of earshot.

"What are you up to, Helen?"

"None of your business, please leave the office."

"But this is our office . . . and that is our phone. What's going on?"

"I have to make a very important and confidential call and Yves does not trust the extension phone that we have in our workshop. He says that Jim Simpson would let us use his private line. We cannot have anyone overhearing."

Even at my tender age I already knew better than to argue with an angry woman and let her get on with her important call. After she had finished and calmed down a little she did allow us a little information that she was passing on some critical data to an unnamed client in London regarding the results of a Schlumberger test on a recent North Sea well. All this added to the intrigue and the various rumours in circulation.

I had only limited knowledge of Geology but recognised straight away that the BP core samples were from carboniferous zones and that the 150 (approximately) four-foot sections amounted to a considerable pay-zone. The Geologist had a checklist and was careful to ensure that each sample was properly packed, protected and labelled. Some of the boxes had been loosened in transit and we could see, while repairing those damaged packages, that the core samples had distinct layers of dark rock, which was obviously oil. The boxes identified by the Geologist were sorted into three batches, each of which was destined for delivery to different laboratories for analysis. By the end of the afternoon three separate pick-up trucks arrived to collect the batches. I had been charged with marking up the boxes for Robertson Research, and I recall that the truck picking up those boxes had been instructed to deliver the cargo on a "Hot Shot" basis—i.e. the driver had to drive through the night and deliver his consignment to Robertson Research's base in North Wales by 9am Friday.

The driver was justifiably delighted with the £200 fee that he would earn for his efforts. The Geologist merely smiled and strolled off at closing time as if this had been a routine day. Stanley beamed and chortled as the final truck left and he carefully locked up his store. I remember pocketing the thirty-pence marker pen.

# 7. The Barytes Cutters' Ball

The stormy conditions of the North Sea were well known to local fishermen and the international oil operators and contractors were equally aware of the risks and demands. This was encapsulated in a colour picture advertisement from one of Gulf Publishing's magazines (I think it was "World Oil" and probably for Baldt Anchors) depicting a semi-submersible rig at a precarious angle amidst breaking rollers with the caption;

***That North Sea is a rough mother. . . . . . !***

During the winter of 70-71 there was a lull in the Dubs activity. Only the toughest of units could withstand the much stronger winds, waves and currents, and so the less capable *Glomar III*, *Sonda I* and *Bluewater 3* would be laid up or moved to calmer waters of the Mediterranean and the Gulf of Mexico while the sturdier *Staflo*, *Neptune 7* and *Sea Quest* stayed with their Mother.

With less drilling there was less need for mud and other materials and, although the Shell staff at Market Street usually appeared to be fully occupied, there were times at Regent Road when the equipment lay idle, overtime was cut and pay packets dwindled. I now had time to reconsider my return to University, complete my Thesis and take the Final Exams, but I still had a mental block so my thoughts turned increasingly to alternative employment.

The idea of being a Mud Engineer was quite appealing. Those I had met so far with IMC and Baroid all seemed quite practical, intelligent, and well educated, although only the Americans had University qualifications; mind you, apparently you could obtain a USA degree by spelling your name correctly. They were well rewarded for their efforts, living in West End Houses at £80-£100 per month and going on exotic holidays during their abundant leisure time. They all drove jazzy cars like David James in his Fiat 124 Coupe, Mike Kroeckl in his cute Honda 650 and, newly arrived from Houston, Bob Macnab of Milchem in his gold Jaguar E-Type sporting a personalised number plate with the State of Registration in small blue letters and his surname below in bold red letters:

TEXAS

# MACNAB

Bob was tall, well built and quite handsome, not at all as brash as most Texans were reputed to be, nor as you might guess from his automobile but, nevertheless, he attracted a lot of attention from the media and emerged as something of a celebrity in the growing circus and was henceforth entitled "Texas" Macnab.

I learned from talking to these guys that I could easily complete the three month training programme which all of their companies offered to suitable candidates, but I did not have the £300 to pay for the course nor did I then know of the pact Jim Simpson had with all of the Service Company's clients; this "Gentleman's Agreement" included that he would not disclose any of the confidential information that they entrusted to him and they would not poach any of his staff. Within a year, owing to the drastic shortage of Mud Engineers, the Mud Companies would begin to pay for training and accommodation and I heard from all sorts of sources that they were scouring the globe for candidates but I never received a single offer and so I carried on filling in the XS141, GW10 and OW81 Customs forms and cutting barytes, bentonite, salt and cement for £12 per week.

During the lull in mud shifting operations Jim Simpson diverted our efforts into reclaiming some of the spaces in the old warehouses. The old gatekeeper's lodge fronting on to Regent Road had already been scrubbed up and turned into workable apartments for IMC and Amoco. An Estate Agent would probably describe them as

"Bijou Mews Type Offices." IMC adopted the faintly twee title of "Oak Tree Stores" on their business cards although a hundred years or more would have elapsed since a tree of any kind grew on that site.

The space behind that had been bagged by Mike Robertson, who was equally as well informed and as confident as Jim Simpson on the prospects of Aberdeen developing as the centre of Northern Sector activities, and wanted to replicate the success he had enjoyed in Great Yarmouth with his supply company, Offshore Drilling Supplies Limited. He had moved Peter Marshall to run the ODS Aberdeen show. Jim planned to fill the remainder of the ground floor with offices for our own use. Working on the confidential information gleaned from those senior executive callers that he had entertained during 1967-1970, he knew that by the summer of 1971 he could lease out any warehouse or office space that he could lay his hands on.

As there was little demand for temporary offices, simple economics dictated that there was a very poor supply throughout Aberdeen, but above the ASC and ODS areas lay two floors of vacant floor-space that Jim reckoned could be converted into reasonable cubicle offices. Twelve offices of 200 square foot each on each floor would be ideal for incoming prospectors. In the old decrepit building behind the illuminated "Long John" sign there were a further three floors that could be accessed.

Apart from planning permission (which could take years even if it was finally granted) and a Fire Certificate (which proved negotiable) the only obstacle was the roof-space, then filled with derelict grain mill machinery, heavy iron and steel shafts and pulleys, wood and tin separators, asbestos belts and about two tons of pigeon guano. All that would need to be removed before we could start building the partitions and doors and equipping the new apartments suitable for human occupation—in less than six months!

Under Jimmy Gallan's watchful eye the crew began to dismantle the heaviest pieces, which comprised the electric motors, steel shafts and cast iron bearings that had been used to drive the grain sifting machinery. This was when we learned to appreciate Jock Begg's brute strength and Sandy Scott's guile. Jock would do the sledge-hammer wrecking and Sandy would know how, where and when to apply the crowbar or sack barrow.

After everything had been lowered to ground level we then had to arrange for disposal; this was when Jock Smith would apply his special knowledge. It was fairly common practice for the workmen in most factories, plants and depots to enjoy a share of the spoils in the "Scrap Fund" and, as a goodwill gesture, Jim Simpson had donated the proceeds of the sale of the scrap metal (which was the only material of any worth in the project) to the "Barytes Cutters."

As well as having a good nose for acquiring various items like a "Fry" of fish or a box of nails, Jock Smith always knew the best places to go to obtain the best rates for scrap and so he usually was first choice as the driver taking away the debris. I had the pleasure of riding "Shotgun" with him on a few occasions, ostensibly to help him unload but also to make sure that there was no doubt about the weights and rates agreed. Jimmy Gallan trusted Jock and so did Jim Simpson but some of the others had their doubts and this, after all, was "their" money, so there was to be no "hooghery paghery."

"Scrappy Hey's peyin' £20 a ton for cast but only £15 for steel so we'd better get thon bearin's richt aff the shafts an keep them separate."

"We're nae gaun tae McAtoostie's or Stewart's—they'll skin ye!"

"Dod Douglas'll tak' the motors hale, so nae need tae brak them up."

Jock could tell his metal. Anything with a copper content was extremely valuable and he would usually take as great care as possible to separate as much clean copper wire or plate. Likewise with bronze or alloys. "McAtoostie" was Jock's term for the McAllisters. He said it was something he had picked up on the fishing boats, one of the many and varied jobs he had done over the past twenty years. It was deemed to be unlucky to have a crew-member of that name and if perchance one did appear on board a trawler he would be called by his nickname.

Trawlermen are notoriously superstitious or "Supersuspicious" as Jock pronounced that word. I was never sure whether Jock was clumsy with his diction or deliberately obtuse but he was good fun to be with.His efforts contributed greatly to the "Barytes Cutters" fund and I learned quite a bit about materials in the process.

With the heaviest machinery dismantled and disposed of we set about clearing up the scrap timber and pigeon poo; here there was a clear division of labour. The priority was obviously to get rid of the heavy and valuable scrap metal and the boys set about that task with gusto, but when it came to the rubbish, well that was left to me and "Aul' Jake."

Jake Forbes was one of my favourite people, one of the finest I have had the pleasure to meet. He was also related to me as well as Jim Simpson and I had come across him occasionally at family weddings and New Year parties where he would usually be sat cheerily with a dram in one hand and a pipe in the other. Already into his seventies, he had been given a job as "Sweeper up" at Gordon Graham, where he made sure that all the broken bottles were cleared off the roads, and he had been kept on to make sure that the old dross from the "Coal Hole" did not contaminate the precious drilling mud that now filled the warehouse.

Like most of his generation he had been a farm labourer working the feein' market from Kennethmont to Carnoustie. He had also been a soldier and had served with the "Black and Tans" during the Irish Troubles.

"I focht an' fled fer my country," he would joke.

Sometime in his thirties he had been stricken with tuberculosis, which left him with a severely twisted spine and breathing difficulties, and he had been confined to a wheelchair for several years before, surprisingly and inexplicably, recovering some strength in his legs, enabling him to walk and work again. He had also lost his wife in birth to his daughter, Margaret, but, in all the time that I knew him, I never heard him complain. I heard him curse, for sure, but then only with due cause and always followed with a quip or a laugh.

Although he struggled with stairs and general mobility, he always made himself available and willing to help with tidying up or making tea. From his agricultural background Jake had learned that the simplest way was usually the safest and best way, and he proved to be a wise and helpful journeyman, guiding me in my attempts to master the various implements that we needed to complete the demolition. As I would flail with a sledge-hammer at the shafts and screens that made up the mechanical sifting part of the grain sorting process, Jake would indicate the target point that would yield the maximum purchase. I would heave at the larger pieces of furniture and Jake would sweep up the shards and splinters, pointing out that the finer parts of the machinery were held together by copper nails which he would pick out by claw hammer and deposit carefully in a plastic bucket.

"That'll be worth a shillin' or twa for the Barytes Cutters' Kitty."

It was during this spell of working with Aul' Jake, smashing sledgehammers into grain shafts, pulling wooden slats from aeration vents and dismantling all the old worn paraphernalia that I had what could be described as a moment of Epiphany. Here we had a very simple, straightforward task—remove all the old crap to make way for the new, clear out the obsolete equipment and make space for future development.

There was no abstract conceptualisation such as I faced with Sociology, no thesis, no antithesis or synthesis with vague, half-baked theories and spurious conclusions, just a plain set of instructions and an opportunity to swing the sledge-hammer and knock lumps out of the dead wood. New Age Gurus have sold millions of books, TV programmes and self-help kits extolling the virtues of de-cluttering and starting afresh. High salaried psychotherapists will charge thousands of pounds to recommend just the kind of thing that I worked out for myself in those few weeks working with Jake.

The space that Jake and I cleared would now be described as a Dockside Studio Loft Conversion featuring cast iron cylindrical pillars, natural wooden floors and full height scenic windows. With the impressive harbour views and quaint cobble stoned driveways I imagine that if they had been built as residential apartments they would now be extremely attractive to neo-urban professionals.

Jim Simpson had them laid out as open plan offices, proving ideal as a site for the new Sedco Training School, run by Tommy Bicknell, and later as an Executive Suite for Ashland Oil under the care of Pete Rogers. These offices were completed and filled by January 1972. A higher priority was attached to the cubicle offices at the front of the building as these had been promised to Amoco and Conoco, who had committed to a joint two year drilling operation commencing June 1971. All available resources were dedicated to getting these finished.

Joiners, led by Dick Hogg, would appear at all hours and knock up the partitions in double quick time. There was to be no repeat of the Danny Gibb Saga. Johnny McCall was our sole Electrician and he, too, would appear at the strangest times to run cable and fit switches into the spaces cut out of the plasterboard. Johnny was undoubtedly one of the exceptions to Jimmy Gallan's Rule of "Toonsers and Teuchters."

Although he was obviously of town stock Johnny would work efficiently and tirelessly in all events and conditions and always smilingly and uncomplainingly. He was a Plumber as well as an Electrician but, with the severe shortage of water facilities in the old building, he did not have much work to do in that respect. Additional water supplies could have been sought but that would probably have alerted the authorities to the extent of the building work being performed at Regent Road. The lack of adequate toilet and food preparation facilities would prove to be a common source of complaint among the incoming tenants, most of who would have been used to more salubrious surroundings, but I think this relative hardship helped to engender a sort of community spirit, a kind of "Blitz Bonhomie."

In his more expansive moments Jim Simpson would speak of his dream of providing the full range of accommodation and services that the incoming hordes of multinational oil companies would require. He called it his "Happy Valley Project" and he had already identified a suitable site at Middleton Farm to the south of Aberdeen on the land now comprising East Tullos upon which he would build fully surfaced pipe-yards, secure and watertight warehouses and offices with central heating, air-conditioning and proper rest rooms, gymnasia even.

Among the regular visitors to Jim's newly upgraded Executive Suite, was the dashing and adventurous Alan Minto, of Leo Durnin Minto and Strachan, the leading firm of architects in Aberdeen. Another was the pleasant and patient David Young of F G Burnett, the quantity surveyors. I could tell from the brief discussions I had with these fellows while they waited to be admitted or while watching over their shoulders (as I brought them tea or coffee in the Executive Suite) at the carefully detailed blueprints on the desk of the that there was real substance to Jim Simpson's vision. This was no pipe-dream.

I can also confirm, after double checking with the people who were the decision makers at the multinational oil companies (invariably well-positioned, pragmatic but approachable guys,) who had beaten a path to the door of Aberdeen Service Company, that Jim Simpson and his Property Professionals had interpreted perfectly their demands and aspirations and would have enjoyed their patronage for years to come—had we been able to deliver.

These guys at Amoco, Conoco, et al had seen that, since 1967, starting from scratch and in spite of severe obstacles provided by a myopic Harbour Board, a recalcitrant Dock Labour Board, an uncaring local Council, limited financial resources, inadequate infrastructure and an inexperienced workforce, Aberdeen Service Company had delivered a high quality response to the most obscure demands and, generally, understood their business.

The problem remained that the decisions as to how to allocate the necessary resources toward achievement of the joint aims of the Service Company and their valued and valuable clients lay with these obstacular bodies. Aberdeen Harbour Board looked only at the revenues generated on a tonnage basis from the chief users—fishing, forestry, shipbuilding and paper; AHB regarded Oil Exploration as a nine day wonder.

Aberdeen was a relatively small port and the lack of scale was carried over into a lack of ambition. Dock labour operations were run under the control of John Cook & Sons, an old established family outfit, firmly rooted in the past. Cook's regarded Aberdeen Service Company as pumped-up parvenus. Aberdeen City Council, controlled by the Labour Party, was not noted for supporting innovation and the Happy Valley Project was batted back and forth for years until Jim's eager clients were forced into alternative plans.

Problems also arose from suppliers and contractors. As a relatively young company, Aberdeen Service Company did not have a credit record. Jim Simpson, for all his smooth talking and high ambitions was not an established name within the city and obtaining credit from suppliers of plant and equipment, construction work and services was becoming increasingly difficult. I recall an occasion when I had been sent to fetch protective clothing for working on one of our bulk-cutting operations. Working with caustic soda was dangerous and also very damaging to natural fabrics. We needed some nylon overalls to protect our normal clothes and I was despatched to the local supplier, Cosalt, with orders to pick up half a dozen pairs in various sizes. I rushed to their Market Street shop and confidently dictated our requirements to the counter assistant. He seemed pleased enough to find and furnish these items but came across a bit snooty when I suggested that he charge it to the Asco account.

"Sorry, sonny, this will have to be paid cash."

"How much is it for six boiler suits?"

"That'll be ten pounds and eighty pence."

I was astonished that a business of Cosalt's standing needed to insist on a cash payment for such an insignificant amount but their "coonter-louper's" attitude was not untypical. There were some notable exceptions, however, and I am pleased to recount the enterprising and accommodating approach of John Williams of Typewriter Services (Aberdeen) Ltd when we subsequently went searching for all manner of office equipment for the wave of incoming clients. Everybody benefited from that and I was gratified to observe, over the years, how John's outfit blossomed into the TYSEAL empire while Cosalt stagnated.

Amoco eventually built their own facility in East Tullos and Conoco moved to Dundee. In the short term they fitted in along with several others like American Coldset Corporation, Sub Sea International, Vetco and Rankin Kuhn all attracted by the strengthening rumours of a Klondyke into the hastily assembled offices and warehouses that came to comprise the Regent Road Complex.

In spite of the tight schedule and all the extraneous problems relating to the building, outfitting and staffing, the Complex was completely full and operating happily by the summer of 1971. This was exceptional given that the new arrivals came from a wide range of nationalities and backgrounds. The nationalities were easy to detect from their names and accents but social standing was impossible to discern as most of the newcomers adopted a casual, informal approach, which made for easy acquaintance and a remarkably comfortable *modus operandi.*

This came as a refreshing change to the beak-sniffing pomposity and hierarchical rigidity of typical British business relations. The Sedco Christmas Party was a fine illustration. Sedco was the Drilling Contractor who had arrived at Regent Road in June '71, engaged by Amoco and Conoco, paying something like $2 million Mobilisation Fee and a rate of $20,000 per day to haul their semi-submersible rig halfway round the world from New Zealand to the North Sea, in order to fulfil their ambitious exploration programme;

94

a big, successful, wealthy organisation whose assets and incomes would dwarf the strongest local companies.

At this financial level any normal person would excuse them for keeping their own highly privileged company and spending their significant but hard earned money in opulent seclusion but Sedco, under the amiable and inclusive management style of the venerable Elmer Adkins, preferred to share their festive joy with everybody who had helped them settle into their new life in a new location. This included customers (existing and potential,) their rig hands on "off-time," all of their office and warehouse staff, and all of Aberdeen Service Company's staff (even me.)

All of the other tenants in the Regent Road Complex would also be invited to the party. This was eye-opening hospitality, especially as the party was held at the Tree Tops, the most exclusive and expensive hotel in Aberdeen in '71. We all had a wonderfully relaxed evening, appreciating the informality as much as the fine food and wine.

By the end of '71, as a result of Aul' Jake's careful gathering of paper sacks from the mud cutting and Jock Smith's negotiations on sales of scrap metal, we had built up a decent fund in the "Kitty." We began to consider what could be done by way of a celebration. We had enough money for a Dinner Dance or similar but not enough people. We could have had a night out on the beer but, as some of the lads lived in the more remote parts of Aberdeenshire, there would be problems in getting everyone home safely. It was Maggie Simpson's idea to hire a bus and she offered to pay as long as she got to choose where we would go on a Magical Mystery Tour. This was warmly received and, with the undertaking that the "Kitty" would cover the costs of the food and drink en route, we made plans for a day trip on the next Aberdeen Public Holiday Weekend.

After picking up the "Toonsers" from Regent Road, and several "Teuchters" at points along the way, we headed for the Gordon Arms in Huntly for Morning Coffee before taking the heather-strewn Highland route over the Cabrach to Aviemore for lunch and a look round and back via The Lecht to Balmoral (so that it could be described as a "Royal" Tour) ending up at the old cinema in Banchory, which had been converted into a Bar/Restaurant/ Discotheque where we dined, drank and danced the night away.

The Magical Mystery Tour proved to be a roaring success and a well-received morale booster. The only problem, apart from Rosemary McSherry breaking the heel of her platform boots while boogying to Hawkwind's "Silver Machine," was that Maggie and Jim had paid for everything. None of us had to put our hand in our pockets the whole day and they dismissed any suggestion of accepting a contribution from the "Barytes Cutters Fund.. Naturally, this was gratefully received and appreciated, but it meant that we still had about £300 unspent from the "Kitty" and we had to start thinking what we could do with it. Alex Forbes and Merv McIntyre, with their experience in organising entertainment events at The Students Union and Graeme Thomson, with his pretensions to sophistication were appointed to go away and think about some ideas for another party. The only conditions we laid down were that:

Everybody in the Regent Road Complex would be invited, we had to spend every penny in the "Kitty," and it had to be as much fun as the magical Mystery Tour.

We were now well into the 1972 Drilling Season and more rigs had arrived, demanding more consumables, which meant that many more sacks were to be cut and re-cycled. There was some sort of paper shortage, which led to a significant rise in the price fetched for scrap paper. Our outlet at Davidson's still had not twigged why a lorry load of our torn paper sacks would weigh twice as much as any other similar sized load. Jock Smith, in his inimitable fashion, would explain that these were higher quality, double strength paper liners designed for the extraordinary demands of the offshore oil industry, not caring to mention the formidable weight of the residual barytes sticking to the corners. Our kitty was boosted by donations from Amoco and Conoco, who allowed us to take away their worn out drilling bits and other metal returned from the rig.

96

Alex, Merv and Graeme had worked on keeping costs down by hiring private rooms rather than a hotel. By bringing in a caterer, buying the drink on "Sale or Return" basis and providing our own entertainment, (Alex ran a mobile discotheque in conjunction with Hughie Webster of Sedco and Fergus Dodds of Rainbow Printers, who was also persuaded to provide the tickets and menus) we would comply with the regulations for earning a "Late Licence" allowing us to continue to serve drink until 1am.

And so "The Barytes Cutters' Ball" was planned for the Hazlehead Tea Rooms with 140 guests, a three course meal, a temporary bar and "Humphrey Disco." We had calculated that our Kitty would cover the cost of the rooms the dinner and the first couple of drinks and that everyone would be paying their own way after about nine o'clock. This was the message we conveyed as we hand-delivered the printed invitation to all the "Barytes Cutters" and to all our favoured guests, purposely including everyone in the Regent Road Complex, the guys who had helped with the building and outfitting, the part-time cleaners and even the friendly local policemen, Neil and Gerry, who could generally be dissuaded from issuing parking tickets by the provision of a cup of coffee (and a biscuit.)

Everyone, that is, apart from Charlie Moberly. Charlie was the top man at Sun Oil who had occupied the North West Corner Suite for a few months but, in that time he had failed to make a single friend. His moaning, supercilious demeanour had alienated his staff, his suppliers, his neighbours and his wife who was, allegedly, equally grumpy. He even earned a rare parking ticket from Neil the Bobby. He may have reckoned that as the UK Boss of this prestigious major oil company he did not need to curry favour and that everyone should bend to his will. This is a disturbingly common trait among some of the senior executives that I have encountered in many years of business and I assume it comes from low self-esteem and insecurity.

Whatever the psychological analysis or other explanation, none of us could summon up the false charm that would have been necessary to extend an invitation to Charlie to join us at the "Barytes Cutters' Ball." We did not have to justify the "non-invitation," as it was the "Barytes Cutters" fund, and it was for them and their new friends to enjoy. Charlie had contributed nothing to the fund nor to the generally good nature that pervaded Regent Road, and we did not want to risk losing the fun factor. Unsurprisingly, he took umbrage and carried his grievance firstly to Kenny Mann, our new General Manager, who pleaded ignorance. He then bleated to Jim Simpson, who successfully placated this piqued patron in his most suave, elegant, sycophantic prose, explaining that the choice was out of his hands and, anyway, this would be an unattractive event to someone of Charlie's *savoir-faire*.

One of our preferred clients, and a man accepted at Regent Road as the affable, experienced and knowledgeable gentleman that he invariably would be to all who met him, was Bill Byatt. Bill was an independent Contractor working on Conoco's behalf as Materials Co-ordinator. He called the shots (and approved the bills) on all the logistics and material transactions relating to Conoco's involvement in the *Sedco 135F* drilling programme.

He was a key man and, by nature of his position and perceived power, it would be understandable if he, too, had adopted the Charlie Moberly approach to suppliers and sub-contractors, but, as those of us who got to know him will attest, he was always a gentleman and treated everyone with proper respect and genuine humanity. When we extended our invitation to Bill to join us at the "Barytes Cutters' Ball," he offered his immediate and grateful acceptance. He then enquired, graciously as always, how these boys, the barytes cutters, could afford to throw a party of any kind. This was unprecedented in his extensive experience. We explained the background to the funding, which Bill picked it up appreciatively, but we were floored by his response:

"This is a fabulous idea. All over the world I go to look after various Oil Companies' materials and I end up in some pretty exotic places and get all sorts of entertainment and offers (a wink and a nod was sufficient to describe the temptations that await the distributors of oil exploration funds) but I've never heard of such of thing before. Your "Barytes Cutters" who work like blazes, as I've seen, but probably don't earn very much, as I presume, are prepared to share their little bit of scrap money that they've picked up over a year with people they've only just met. That's astonishing! I'm humbled."

He then produced an envelope, which we were to discover contained £200, and asked us to put that towards the fund and ensure that everyone would have a drink after dinner at the Ball. Bill also explained that he had been given this money by the Captain of one of the Smit Lloyd supply boats working on the same project, who had retrieved an anchor chain which had been discovered during a rig move earlier that year.

The Captain and crew were entitled to the Salvage Rights on the chain, as there was no proof of ownership. They had required Bill's assistance in obtaining berthing facilities to offload the chain at a scrapyard in Peterhead. Whatever they received from Northern Shipbreakers is unknown, but Bill had been given this package as his "share." Many in his position would have simply pocketed the proceeds and said no more but Bill, we surmised, had higher principles. He was also a practical man and knew, from experience, that, if he had tried to go through the proper procedures in reporting this incident and accounting for the money, even with a fairly pragmatic organisation like Conoco, he would have to write so many reports and fill in forms, the exercise would prove cumbersome and distracting. He, therefore, made the magnanimous and probably correct decision to donate the money to the Barytes Cutters. Top Man!

We now had enough money to ensure that all would be fed and watered and so we concentrated on the entertainment, making sure that Humphrey Disco had music to suit all nationalities, ages and preferences; this could not be just a Glam Rock Thrash! As things turned out, we did not need the Disco for, about an hour after the Dinner, as Hughie was working his "Patter" and spinning the platters and we all were warming up for a bit of jigging, there was a power cut plunging us into darkness. It's funny how often a party is enhanced by an unexpected break in proceedings and, with a couple of beers or Sweet Martinis under our belts, we were in fairly good humour. The trouble was that without music and dancing people started to down their drinks more quickly than anticipated and, by nine o'clock our Kitty was severely depleted.

I am unsure whether anyone mentioned this to anyone in particular but, out of the blue, Ronnie Graver of Milchem announced that his boss, Bob "Texas" Macnab had instructed him to pay £100 towards the party and, as he had his company chequebook with him, he duly signed it off and handed it over to Dod Gibb, who was as usual in charge of the bar. This was gratefully received and tided us over until about ten o'clock.

Someone managed to unearth a piano, which was wheeled out and dusted off. We had a selection of "Ivory Tinklers" in the ranks and were variously amused by Jim Simpson's Boogie Woogie and others' equally enthusiastic renditions. One of the players (I'm sorry I cannot recall which,) had a workable repertoire of Scottish Tunes and as these were reeled off there were impromptu lessons conducted in the authentic performance of "Gay Gordons," "Strip the Willow," and "Dashing White Sergeant." My own view is that an Eightsome Reel is not legitimate unless at least one of the participants is conveyed horizontally or ejected from the reel in the manner of an All-In Wrestler and this much was achieved fairly soon as our American friends adapted marvellously to this new fangled dancin'. The party was in full swing when Jimmy Gallan, as enthusiastic at jigging as he is at anything demanding physical effort, mentioned to Gaines Garland, the new IMCO Manager who was clearly enjoying his evening, that, in the interests of Fair Play he ought to ask Dick Cotton if he could match Milchem's generous donation.

"Sure!" Gaines drawled as he mopped his brow, adjusted his wispy ginger "Combover," loosened his green Paisley Pattern shirt, adjusted his green and yellow striped Kipper Tie and hitched up his green houndstooth flared Leisure Pants. "There's enough Big Wheels at this Hootenanny to fill my Expense Account for three months so it should fly. Lemme go check with Cotton first."

With that Gaines took off to find a payphone, called Dick at home in Great Yarmouth, immediately receiving the expected confirmation, and returned very soon brandishing a broad smile and a billfold that would choke a drainpipe. As he began proceeding to peel off the notes, Jimmy held his arm and cautioned him to "haud his horses."

Jimmy wanted to make sure that IMCO's charitable act would be witnessed by his rival from Baroid, the notoriously parsimonious Bob Pate. Had Joe Whittlesey been able to attend the Ball we were all sure that he would have offered his contribution without question but Bob's suit was cut from a more tightly woven cloth and he was going to require a little persuasion. He did not rise to the bait of Gaines Garland's wad waving nor did he seem to appreciate the uniqueness of this marketing opportunity or the simple gesture of rewarding his loyal hard working Barytes Cutters. It was only when Jimmy and I blackmailed him by suggesting that we would call Joe ourselves and ask for his blessing that he relented.

"All right, y'all got me this time. I'll belly up to the bar, but I don't have that kind of cash on me right now (he never did.) I'll give you my "Marker," can I pay ya Monday?"

We took his handwritten marker and gave it Dod Gibb behind the the bar who opened it, read it quickly, then scoffed, loudly, so that everyone could hear;

"An IOU fae Bob Pate? Ah micht as weel wipe ma erse wi it!"

Bob laughed as loud as any but then hurried off to the same payphone to check with his boss that his promise would be covered. He returned with a smile wider than Gaines Garland's, wider than the Mississippi River and proudly proclaimed;

"Joe Whittlesey's paying for all the drinks until the bar closes!"

The late licence, which had been arranged until 1 am, was now redundant. As all the drinks were effectively paid for, there was no restriction on the continuing servings and we could continue as long as we wanted. We managed to persuade the Council Caretakers to stay on (they were enjoying this party also) and, unsurprisingly, we just about drank the bar dry such that the only returns were a half case of Sweetheart Stout and a bottle of Bols Advocaat; which is about the same as a typical Scottish New Year.

By four in the morning most people had had enough of the drinking, dancing, singing and capering. Aul' Jake had fallen into the ornamental goldfish pond and had to be rescued. Some young lovers had disappeared into the woods (to explore Nature, we presume) and sufficient sensible folks had even managed to stay sober enough to drive others home. Jimmy Gallan was one of those and he piled about eight of us into the back of his Hillman Hunter Estate, dropping us off to the sound of rattling milk floats.

As successful as the "Barytes Cutters Ball" undoubtedly was, and people of all persuasions would recount their memories of the occasion for several years afterwards, there was to be no repeat. From then onwards it transpired that the individual companies would organise their own events, and would invite only their clients and/or their staff, and though the locations, the food, the wine, the entertainment would be on a grander scale, not one of any of the subsequent parties would match the unique communal spirit of "The Barytes Cutters' Ball."

*1. Jimmy Gallan in his trademark boiler suit and black beret alongside Maitland Simpson leaving their grubby marks on the boss's sleek new Jaguar XJ6. Seated in the car is the ever patient Maggie Simpson.*
*Photo by Jim Simpson.*

*2. Jock Smith – a rough sketch. Jock was not particularly photogenic.*

*3. The Kit. Sketches of the "Papper Up" (Elevator), Auger, Cutting Table and Bulker. Total investment less than £500.*

*4. At the table. A close-up of the action at the cutting table. Notice: no gloves, masks or goggles.*

*5. Cutting Barytes. The introduction of the Auger was a step forward.*

*6. Brine Tank at Pocra Quay. Sending Salt Water to the North Sea? Are you serious?*

*7. Sea Quest, Spider Deck. This is similar to the spider deck on Sedco 135F as described in the action in Chapter 4 "Influx" and gives some indication of the harsh working environment. Courtesy of BP Archive, Warwick University.*

*8. Shamrock FC Dinner Dance, Royal Hotel, Feb 1970. Back Row: Jim McPherson, Davie Merson, Johnny Milne, Alan Merson, Davie Wright, Walter Baxter, Alan McLaughlin, Johnny Middleton, Bill Forsyth. Front Row: Jim Hamilton, Bill Davidson, Ian Leslie, Jim Milne, Bryan Mowat, Davie McEwen.*

*9 .Sedco 135F - Waiting on Weather. Courtesy of J L Daeschler*

*10. Hermes at Cove Thistle Feb 1972. Back Row: Alex N. Forbes, Fred Dalgarno, Les Hutton, Les Dalgarno, Paul McHugh, Dennis Wyness. Front Row; Alan McDonald, Sandy Reid, Ian Hogg, John Milne, Les Bowie.*

11. *New Bulker. Bought with £17,000 of Sidlaw's money, this new-fangled piece of machinery could not handle as much as the old bulker which was picked up for a pittance. But then it was designed by a committee.*

12. *Elmer Adkins on a trip to Lerwick to persuade Capt. Inkster to allow them to develop a rig inspection and repair facility in Bressay Sound. Nothing resulted from the idea. Shetland had bigger fish to fry.*

# 8. Wheels

Along with their wedding day and the birthdays of their spouse and children, most people remember the day they passed their driving test. With my (usually) reliable memory I have yet to forget an anniversary or miss a family birthday although some "jogging" may have been required along the way. Tuesday 18th August 1972, 2.30pm, outside the Ashgrove office of the Ministry of Transport is etched on my brain and will never be removed. It was at that hour on that day that Her Majesty's representative of the Aberdeen MOT Driving Examination Centre came close to being a victim of Jimi Hendrix's exhortation from "Purple Haze."

*"Excuse me while I kiss this guy!"*

As he conveyed the coveted "pink slip" that particular driving test examiner was saved from a horrible fate not only by his drab features and abject lack of a sense of humour but also by my eagerness to rush off and tell all my mates and colleagues of my success. Skipping down Ashgrove Road on to Berryden Road I looked up at the puffy white clouds, held the pink slip to my mouth and kissed the sky (which I think is what Hendrix actually said and to which no stuffy driving examiner could object).

It was not just the relief of obtaining a full driver's licence (at the third attempt) nor the glee of passing an examination, although I had not had not experienced any of those since abandoning University two years hither, nor enjoying a Rite of Passage, as no memorable ceremony was involved. This was, however, a passport to all sorts of possibilities. I began to list all the plusses as I boarded the No. 17 bus for Torry and back to work at Regent Road.

There would be no more trudging back and forth between our office in Aberdeen Docks and my flat in Holburn Street. There would be no rush to catch the last bus back to town after taking my girlfriend home to Culter. Even better, there would be no trudging eight miles back to Aberdeen having watched the Bluebird Bus flying by the stop at the foot of Bellenden Brae at 10.52 three minutes ahead of its schedule. I could join the elite band of amateur footballers and drive to games rather than taking a Corporation Bus to Hazlehead or Inverdee. There would be no need to cadge a lift off a team-mate who would, invariably, hit you for "petrol money."

In a moment of generosity (or grandiosity) Jim Simpson had promised a company car to each of his "key" men at Aberdeen Service Company. Jimmy Gallan, who had almost single-handedly built the fabric and reputation of the outfit, had been rewarded with a brand new white Hillman Hunter Estate—PRS 779 J. The rest of us were too young and naïve to have had the opportunity to contribute anything of any significance towards the success of the organisation but, in the heady spirit of burgeoning enterprise, we had each carved out a niche of sorts.

Alex Forbes had joined us in June 1971 after graduating as MA at the University of Aberdeen. As Jim Simpson's half brother Alex had a bit of an "inside track" on the future growth prospects of the company and, with his unstinting ambition (and a valid driving licence) he had jumped at the opportunity of learning the ropes as a Ship's Agent, shuttling to and fro between our office and the supply boats on Pocra Quay and out to the Heliport at Dyce to check the loading and offloading of materials as well as looking after the Master's requirements.

Within a year Alex was our self-titled "Shipping Manager" and was readily prepared to hector big brother for the right to a company car. Graeme Thomson had abandoned his studies at RGIT as a Quantity Surveyor and had joined shortly after Alex. He too could drive and had dabbled in the shipping side but never quite displayed any of the urgency that is a prerequisite in that field. As I could not drive it was presumptuous to indulge any fanciful hopes of any car.

Office leasing and furnishing were increasingly important to customer satisfaction and growing sources of revenue at ASC.

Neither Alex nor I had shown any interest in these areas, so Graeme had taken on the tasks of chasing for desks, typewriters and toilet rolls and other paraphernalia and subsequently adopted the mantle of "Property Manager," tagging on to Alex's coat-tails in the pursuit of "company wheels."

Aberdeen Service Company, in its original form, was a small family organisation with little capital backing and constantly stretched cash reserves. We did have an impressive portfolio of customers with several major oil companies, Shell, BP, Amoco, Arco, Ashland, Conoco, Sun and Unocal as well as the leading service companies and contractors such as Halliburton, Schlumberger, Sedco, Smedvig and Vetco all queueing up to use any services and facilities that we could provide.

As I have written previously, the expansion of *our* company (after two years of hard word and several harrowing experiences, I did feel a great deal of loyalty and attachment to The Service Company) in the provision of those services and facilities depended on the understanding and co-operation of the Harbour Board, Aberdeen City Council, Customs & Excise, Government Development Agencies (NESDA) and the banks, all of whom, in varying degrees, over the five years since 1967, had issued platitudes and promises of prosperity, but mostly had delivered nothing but provisos and penalties.

Competitors had moved in to steal our thunder. Those who had shared in the successes of Great Yarmouth and Hartlepool, Hudsons, Offshore Marine and Rankin Kuhn for example, had transferred key personnel such as Malcolm Bradshaw, Roger Baxter and Mike Isbell to Aberdeen to seek out premises and handling facilities for their existing customers.

Local worthies including Graeme Alexander and Ian Wood, with the sound financial backing of their successful parents (Charles Alexander and John Wood respectively) were venturing, belatedly, into the market and they appeared to enjoy better results with the local authorities in securing prime sites and quicker approval of development schemes. By 1972 all of these outfits had established operations and people in place in comparable positions to Alex, Graeme and myself running about the harbour, the pipe-yards and warehouses in liveried Ford Escorts, Vauxhall Vivas and Hillman Avengers. Although I would admit to being slightly envious I have never considered it "cool" to be seen driving any sort of car with the company logo on the side. But then again wheels are wheels and driving a Dagenham Dustbin or a Ryton Write-Off is no joy but sure beats walking.

By way of Alex's inside track we had been putting pressure on Jim Simpson to deliver on his promise of providing company cars. Jim had recently traded in his sleek Jaguar XJ6 for a stunning saluki bronze Citroen SM, a left-hooker with a futuristic dashboard, a cockpit out of Star Trek, space-age seats in mustard Dralon, air conditioning, hydro-pneumatic suspension, variable power steering, directional headlights and a straight-six Maserati engine that sounded as sweet as Sam Cooke singing with The Soul Stirrers.

We had somehow wangled an invitation to the trade launch of this spectacular supercar at Malcolm Ewen's Carden Motors showroom in Albert Place and, as the technically minded gawped over the SM and its equally attractive predecessor, the DS, Alex, Graeme and I mingled on the periphery, munching the cheese and canapes, slurping on the free wine and dreaming of the day when we could afford to buy and drive such things of beauty.

Ever since I was a wee boy I had been an admirer of Citroen. The quirky Traction Avant driven by Maigret, Georges Simenon's fictional French sleuth, displayed a certain panache that put the British counterparts in their hulking Humbers in the shade. Due to its complexity and relatively high price the DS was a rare sight on our roads but was the choice of discerning professionals such as surgeons and architects. The asking price for the SM was well above £5000 while the variants of the DS were in the £2500-£3000 range. Well out of our league.

On the wall and strewn along the display tables Citroen had placed pictures and had placed brochures describing the soon to be introduced GS Model which looked like a smaller version of the deified DS. Between munches and slurps we pointed at the shiny publicity shots and thumbed through the glossy pamphlets. The GS appeared as a very handsome but practical machine and an attractive alternative to the bog standard British Leyland 1100/1300 or the omnipresent Ford Escort.

One of the ever-attentive salesmen spotted our interest and sidled in with his well-practised pitch. After working out who we were and why we were there he got on with his job of trying to promote his product. He had already figured that he need not waste time discussing the "Stars of the Show" and he sideswiped our inane questions on the comparative merits of the SM and DS before spouting his spiel on the imminent arrival of the GS.

On hearing that this model would be available in a few months and would probably be in the £1200-£1600 price range we hummed and thrummed and started to imagine that these were what Jim Simpson was planning to provide as our junior executive transport. I imagined that we had all arrived at this conclusion. We nodded silent glances of approval and concurrence to each other and started to muse. Yes, this was it. Jim had invited us along to show off his protégés to the assembled hordes of local businessmen and dignitaries. Aberdeen Service Company was going places and the pioneering path was going to be led by his hand-picked team of budding executives (Alex, Graeme and me) driving around in shiny Citroen GS variants.

In our hubristic fantasy we had even re-branded ourselves as "Asco." The full title "Aberdeen Service Company" sounded cumbersome and over elaborate when we answered the phone and we needed something snappier and zestier to reflect the growing potential and internationalisation of the business.

Alex and I had had a "brainstorming" session over a cup of tea and a cake one evening while waiting for Jim Simpson to arrive for some meeting (Jim was invariably late for meetings.) We had been considering the acronym "ASC" but had dismissed that as passé. All the big, boring corporations like ICI and IBM featured the dreaded three-letter format. We wanted to be different, vibrant, thrusting. We were the leaders in this fascinating fledgling North Sea Oil adventure. We had considered "Ascoil" but dismissed that as sounding clumsy. Jimmy Gallan also thought this sounded like a headache tablet.

We wanted to sound sleek and responsive and had were debating the merits and demerits of "Asco" when Jim appeared and immediately caught on to the topic of discussion. He thought that "Asco" sounded just right and from then on that is what we called ourselves. We could invent job titles for ourselves and "hip" names for our company. We were entitled to imagine that we would have our choice of company cars and in this environment we were fairly pleased that Jim had brought us along to enjoy the thrill of the debut of these exciting new vehicles for our vaunting ambition. A gleaming GS seemed just the right image for our hopes.

It was then that the suave salesman sunk our soaring suppositions. Without a hint of irony and with no idea of how high we had pitched our aspirations for corporate transport he beckoned us to follow him into the adjoining showroom where he would show us the cars Jim Simpson had picked out for his Young Turks. With a glassful of Beaujolais, a mouthful of Brie and a headful of eager anticipation I strode confidently ahead of Alex and Graeme, imagining the envious glowers that would come from the Hudson Freight and Offshore Marine guys in their routine repmobiles as they gawped at the Asco boys in their gleaming new Citroen GS voitures.

Opening the sliding partition the salesman uttered a cliched introduction like "Voila," or "Ooh-la-la," or something similar. It might as well have been "Hoop-la," for there in front of us we saw not a sneak preview of a sexy GS in glossy red but a Dyane in dead-dog grey. Those of you who know their cars will be laughing already but for those that do not have that knowledge let me just say that the Citroen Dyane looked like an expanded version of the carton designed to contain Camembert and, from my later experience, drove in much the same fashion.

It was of very simple construction, designed to cope with the cobbled streets and bumpy lanes of rural France, where body panel parts are easily dented and need to be replaced readily and cheaply. There were engine variants of 400 and 600cc. 600cc! That's about the volume of a decent bottle of beer, barely enough to propel a cheese-box with picnic chairs and a folding canvas roof. These were cars for Provencal peasants, not for thrusting North Sea Oilmen. In our collective chagrin we blustered some sort of gratitude to the bemused car salesman and moved toward the far end of the showroom where we huddled together and hastily devised Plan B.

One of the various facilities that Asco had provided for the incomers was an economical car rental service, a prototype of "Rent-A-Wreck." Jim Simpson had foreseen that whereas the senior managers would be provided with top of the range executive saloons and bugger the expense, the junior officials and quite a number of offshore based guys with short term contracts and high disposable income would be seeking low cost cars that they could hire for a few weeks or months.

Jim's marketing nous proved to be spot-on as the influx of Sedco rig hands swarmed all over us to snap up the nearly new wagons at £55 per month. Jim's choice of car, however, was wider of the mark as he had plumped for picking up the six-month old models passed on (at a "bargain price" according to Jim) after their initial rental period with Mitchell's Self Drive. As any racing driver will tell you "Nothing handles as good as a rental car," and it was obvious that Jim's Bargain Buys had been broken in by Jackie Stewart and Emerson Fittipaldi.

As a further contribution to a misguided business decision the chosen cars were British Leyland's Austin 1100 and 1300 models, which, in the tradition of all things British at that time, fell apart with monotonous regularity. We were beleaguered by customer complaints and call-outs to rescue Kiwis and Canadians stranded somewhere out in the wilds of Deeside and Donside with broken gearboxes or seized engines. To cope with the demands of maintaining the fleet of hire cars we had hired another mechanic.

Our stalwart Hebbie Spence was becoming manic keeping up with repairs on the "bargain" flatbeds and bulker trucks that Jim had acquired for the mud operations, and George Kinghorn came to join us.

George was an extremely placid and methodical chap (in contrast to Hebbie, who I think was eventually adopted as the model for "Beaker" in the Muppets,) and he was given the task of keeping the car rental fleet in operation. It could never be a profitable venture as the prices had been pitched at too low a level but, ever mindful of our guiding principle as the premier service company we had an obligation to keep all our customers satisfied.

Alex immediately formed an alliance with George, assuming another new job title as Transport Manager, helping him to devise wall charts and planning schedules that lasted about a week before being abandoned in the face of flat panic, as we were engulfed by the wave of ailing Austins. Over the six months that it took to eventually overcome the various problems, replacing clutches, carburettors, suspension pods, steering boxes and exhausts, we found our valued customers had voted with their brake pedals and had taken their business elsewhere leaving, Asco with a surplus of unsellable, unleasable, but by now surprisingly reliable motors.

As our customers did not want them we had plenty opportunities to test-drive them and found that they were perfectly suited to our needs for driving around the harbour and out to the airport, and we started using them as runabouts. With all the vibrations from driving on the granite setts of the harbour roads the windows would fall out and the exhaust would rattle a bit but we learned to adapt to these minor deficiencies. This is how we got to Plan B.

Following our foray to Carden Motors and faced with the prospect of driving shamefacedly in a pastel shaded Citroen Dyane, Alex exercised all the powers due to his status as a Transport Manager and assumed control of the most roadworthy of the surplus fleet—a white Austin 1300, ORG 434H. From his inside information he had learnt that George, in repairing this particular car, had fitted parts from an uprated version of the marque making this, effectively, a GT

110

Model. It went like shite off a shovel! Graeme consistently pleaded his case for parity, claiming the need to chauffeur clients to airports and hotels, and commandeered the more luxuriously appointed but smaller-engined Austin 1100 in a fetching Turquoise—ORS 211H. As I was still a non-driver, all I could imagine was that, when I did eventually pass the driving test, I would be left with one of the less desirable remnants of our fleet.

My working week consisted of compiling Customs forms for Shell, Sedco and others. Given a choice and with suitably developed management skills I would have delegated the tedious, mind–numbing duties on to others. I remember that I did try but discovered that Alex's handwriting was too atrocious to be accepted and Graeme always had some other more pressing demands and, somehow, never had the time to learn the ropes. As an office-bound non–driver I enjoyed some advantages, in that I was closer to the news and gossip emanating from band of influential incomers concentrated in the rabbit warren that was the Regent Road Complex but that benefit was evaporating as more and more of these were spirited away to their new homes in mushrooming developments in the suburbs and industrial estates. There were demerits also as, being the only spare man available (Alex and Graeme swanning around somewhere) I would be the one to be roped in by Jimmy Gallan to help out if the Barytes Cutters ever got short handed.

I was desperate to get into the more exciting side of our business and my newly acquired driving licence allowed me to realise that dream. The prospect of having to accept the runt of the fleet, a particularly bad example of Longbridge Languor, the last remaining Austin 1100, already beginning to show signs of rust through its dull white exterior, ORS 387H, failed to diminish my enthusiasm as I leapt off the 17 Bus at the Fish Market stop and loped along Commercial Quay towards Regent Road, eager to tell all about my success. You can imagine my astonishment then as I turned into the lane and bumped into Jim Simpson.

"Fit like, loon? You're looking awful pleased with yourself. Have you found a shilling?"

"Naw, Jimmy, I've just passed my driving test!"

"Excellent! I'm looking for a driver but Alex and Graeme are nowhere to be seen. You're just the man, then. What are you doing this afternoon?"

"Oh, I'm just going to tell a'body aboot ma test and try oot thon 1100 on the open road."

"I've a better idea, here, take these keys and fetch Jock's car up to the office door."

Jim threw me the fairly substantial key-bunch with the blue and white logo and pointed me towards Jock Munro's Volvo 144S, an impressive machine, properly designed and built in dark blue painted Swedish Steel with an ergonomic interior, rubber bumpers and Hella foglamps.

"Am I insured tae drive that beast? That's Jock's ain car, is it nae?"

"Well, it *was* Jock's but Asco just bought it, so you're OK to take it."

Without hesitation or further questions I bounded across the cobbles, hopped into the Volvo and sat for a minute amazed at the formidable array of instruments, switches and levers. Although I had only just acquired my licence I had a decent familiarity with the various vehicles from shifting and parking forklifts, flatbeds and broken down cars that lay about the warehouse.

This felt like a "proper" car and I was tickled that my first experience of driving after passing my test should be in such a prestigious motor. I adjusted the seat (Jock Munro was much bigger than me,) put the monster gear lever into neutral, noticing that the clutch was only marginally lighter than that on the Coventry Climax, slotted the substantial key in the starter, stepped on the thumpingly enormous footbrake, and turned the ignition. There was a significantly encouraging roar from the 1986cc twin carburettor engine as I teased the foot-sized accelerator, coaxing the machine into first gear and gingerly creeping along, with the Pirelli Cinturato tyres gripping the cassies across Regent Road down the lane toward the Asco office.

Jim was waiting at the end of the lane and was carefully helping Jock Munro through the doorway. Jock was supporting himself on crutches, his left leg encased in plaster. It transpired that he had taken some kind of fall while out shooting and had broken his leg and was, therefore, incapable of driving. He needed to be taken home and Jim explained that I was to become his dedicated driver until such time that his leg had healed.

I was detailed to take him back to his house on the edge of Stonehaven and pick him up again the next time he was due to come to the office, which would be Thursday. Jock Munro was a giant of a man, about six foot four and seventeen stone of highland granite, strong facial features and a handshake that could crush pomegranates. He looked every inch of the archetypal Toolpusher, which he had been, to considerable success, in the international oil drilling business. I had met him first of all at Shell, where he had been the Drilling Manager and was held in awe by all of his contemporaries and with fawning obedience by many of his subordinates and most of his sub-contractors.

As I got to know Jock I learnt that he did not appreciate obsequiousness, in fact he hated oily creeps; however, after twenty-plus years at Shell he had become inured to them. At heart he was a plain living, clear thinking country boy from Nairn with an aptitude for engineering and a wanderlust that had been satisfied by his travels to Indonesia, Venezuela and other exotic corners of the Petroleum Province. His long stints overseas and high status (Jock was the top dog in the *Staflo* operation that discovered the mighty Brent Field) had earned him the right to retire early on a handsome pension and look forward to a more leisurely life in his beloved homeland pursuing his favourite hobbies of shooting and fishing. Pity about the broken leg! As well as a high pain threshold Jock had a keen, blokeish sense of humour and as I sympathised about his restricted opportunities on the moors and rivers he retorted;

"Bugger the shooting and fishing, this means I winna be able tae get to the Lairhillock!"

The Lairhillock at Netherley was Jock's "local;" about a mile from his house and at that time merely a but 'n ben with a tin roof and an ingle nook. There Jock and his cronies could share a few drams and embellish stories about their experiences; and Jock had more than most.

Asco was continuing to develop its blossoming potential, but due to the limits of Jim Simpson's finances, as well as his acknowledged naivety about the scale of the business, it could not contemplate competing against the might of the Brown & Root and Wimpey (who dominated the service business in Great Yarmouth) or even against the likes of Hudson Freight or Seaforth Maritime who had the ear of the financial organisations.

We also faced new competition from the slow awakening of the prominent Aberdeen Families such as Alexanders (Ariel International) and Woods, who had undoubtedly established wealth but had, to date, shown little interest in this fleeting North Sea Oil caper. It was something of a coup, therefore, to announce to the oil world that the upstart underling scrabbling about Regent Road with a few recycled trucks, ramshackle offices and redundant warehouses had engaged the services of the biggest "wheel."

The envious glances cast by Asco's rivals on the appointment of Jock Munro as our latest recruit were as nothing compared to the green-eyed stares that I detected when I returned from Stonehaven to Regent Road, driving Jock's Volvo and wearing a smile as wide as if I had a slice of melon wedged in my gob. It was nearly five o'clock and, as the offices emptied, there were plenty of parking places so I took the opportunity of parking broadside across the entrance to the coal hole, where I spotted Alex and Graeme lurking sheepishly. They both wore the look of five- year-old cowboys who had been fobbed off with hand-me-down Colt 45's while their bigger brother swanked around with a Winchester '73. Alex tried to mask his envy and play it cool.

"How do you like our new addition to the fleet?"

"Great, Alex, runs like a dream, best car I've driven all day."

Attempts at humour rarely assuage the offended, particularly

114

in the envy stakes, and I imagined Alex's mind angling towards a conclusion that would satisfy his desire to be the King Pin (he was, after all, The Transport Manager and this was a company vehicle) and, at the same time, burst my bubble of pride. In a rare moment of graciousness I decided that gloating would merely lead to confrontation. With the success of my driving test still predominant, and not wishing to allow my special day to be sullied with peevishness, I offered him the keys.

"There you are Alex, have a shottie!"

"Nah, I'll just stick wi' 434H, that's a bit sportier an' it's easier parked. I'm takin Linda tae the Odeon the night. That Volvo widna get in the car park."

"How about you, Graeme? Fancy a birl?"

"No, sorry, I only change my car when the ashtray's full and I've still got a full pack of Dunhills to go through yet. I'll hold on to 211H pro tem."

At that they both turned away, Alex sucking on a Polo Mint to freshen his breath in preparation for his hoped for snogging session, Graeme sucking on an Embassy Regal, which prevented him from cursing my good fortune. Great! Not only had I rattled their cages but I had also been ceded possession of the best car in the fleet, one of the best cars on the road in 1972, and definitely one that caught the attention of all my other friends.

How on earth, I would hear them question, could a boy from a council house in Willowbank Road, a University dropout with only a year or two of work experience and barely a couple of halfpennies to rub together, manage to run about in a top of the range executive saloon? There must be something in this "oil" business lark after all. My responses were generally sanguine and non-committal. I might have spouted something about the rewards for hard work and application which would have been convincing had there been any truth in that but I was not going to blow my new found prestige by telling them that it was all down to good luck and being in the right place at the right time.

More important than the indisputable technical abilities of the

Volvo and the considerable kudos that came my way with it, was the freedom to come and go where I wanted and when I wanted. Going to football was a dawdle; and I saved on bus fares and petrol money. Taking my girlfriend out on her nights off was a cinch. We abandoned the Star & Garter to the growing band of roughnecks and went for hurlies all over the countryside. Overtaking the last bus back from Culter was a particular joy.

At the office I could join in the fun with the other guys and race down to Pocra Quay to deliver a Manifest or roll out to Dyce to pick up incoming VIPs. The extra mobility increased my awareness of some of what was going on. I took trips to Prestwick and Abbotsinch to visit Davidson, Park & Speed (our Import Freight Agents) and saw how the bigger airports were run. I dropped in by Grangemouth and had a close-up look at the BP Refinery. While taking Jock Munro home I would relate my tales of discovery and would listen, attentively, while he regaled me with his account of worldwide oilfield developments.

"You ain't seen nothin' yet! Aberdeen and Yarmouth are nice wee places but nothing like big enough or fast enough to cope wi' what's in the pipeline."

Coming from the man who headed the drilling exploration programme that led to Shell's discovery of the Auk, Brent and Cormorant fields, this had credibility as well as resonance. Jock told me of the vast construction projects that had followed oil exploration successes around the globe. Massive drilling rigs and steel platforms to handle the production and processing, titanic tanks for storage, giant jetties for mooring and loading the oil to super-tankers, each of which would fill Aberdeen Harbour on their own.

"D'ye ken Ardersier?"

"Aye, that's right next tae yer ain place at Nairn, is it nae?"

"Aye, right enaff. Have ye seen it recently?"

"Aye, last year. My girlfriend's Dad took us on a hurlie roon by tae see faur they're gaun tae build the new fabrication yard. There was naethin' there but a few auld caravans."

116

"Hae anither look. Tak' the Volvo up this weekend an' gang in past the Security Guards on the new road they've built. Ye'll see an awfu change. While ye're there ye should tak a trip ower tae Invergordon and Nigg and see what's happenin there."

As luck would have it my girl was off duty that weekend and was back at her folks' place in Forres, about twelve miles from Ardersier, so I took the opportunity to drop by and visit, intent on checking out developments around the Moray Firth. On the Saturday we drove through Inverness and on past Black Isle to Invergordon. The roads were so poor and the traffic so bad that the journey took longer than expected and, by the time we reached Nigg, we did not have enough time for a look around. Well, we might have done, but that would have meant we would have been late back for our dinner so we skipped the inspection tour and headed back for our steak and chips. Even from the briefest of glimpses, however, at the giant construction cranes and the stacks of large diameter steel tubes we could see that something colossal was coming to Cromarty Firth. This proved to become something much bigger than anyone had ever imagined.

Over a succulent steak and chips prepared by Doug Christie, mine-host at the Newmarket Bar in Forres, I listened as he recounted tales of how his pub regulars were ditching their jobs as joiners, bricklayers and welders with local businesses and heading for new openings at the rig yards at twice as much money. Bad news for the local proprietors, good news for the tradesmen, and for Doug. When we dropped in by the pub later that evening the place was hoachin' with young men eager to dispose of their newly acquired riches and buy drinks for everyone, even the incomer who was courting the landlord's daughter. To our pleasant surprise we spotted, holding court in the Lincoln Lounge, our old friend from Aberdeen, Johnny Gorman a footballing legend with Walker Road and East End and sometime joiner.

"Johnny, fit ye daein up this far North?"

"Weil, I was up seeing Jennifer (his girlfriend and, later, wife) in Inverness an I heard McDermotts were hiring at Ardersier. There's nae jinery jobs in Aiberdeen so I thocht I'd hae a look. I got fixed up right awa so I bade on. That's some set up, hae ye seen it yet?"

"Nae yet, Johnny. We had a run up to Nigg this aifterneen. That's impressive."

"Weil, Hi-Fab at Nigg's big an' a' but they're only peyin £50 a wik an I'm getting £55 wi McDermotts. Wi' guaranteed overtime I'm clearin' a hunner a wik!"

"In that case, Johnny, you're buying the drinks."

"Nae bother! Rose, gie's a Bacardi, a Dubonnet and a Black Label. Better mak them doubles, Doug's real stingy wi his nips! Sorry, darlin, I'm forgettin this is yer Da's place. Here, John, you've been in this oil game a while, foo lang d'ye think it'll last?"

My earlier thinking had been that the drilling exercise might be at best a two or three year wave of activity but, with the information that I had gleaned from Jock Munro and other informed sources, I could now contemplate a five year stretch of a mix of industries. Even the wildest and most optimistic projections in the papers, then, extended only to ten or fifteen years.

It was the next day when we took the Volvo on a drive out to Ardersier that my views on the scale of this oil business were confirmed. Avoiding the dangers of the congested A96 we took the back lanes via Dyke and Kintessack, working our way along the coast road to Nairn and looking for the turn off to McDermott's. Seeing a large signpost with the distinctive giant "M" logo I turned right into a little side road before coming to a red and white barrier gate manned by a single chap in a tiny sentry box.

"Ay, ay," I hailed as I rolled down the window.

"Fine day for it," the guard responded in the affable way that Nairn folk greet strangers.

"Any chance of getting in?"

"The yard's closed the day and I'm no supposed tae let anyone in."

"Oh, we're just here for the day and I was hoping for a quick look around."

"Weil, I was telt nae tae let anyone in except Fire, Ambulance or VIP's. Who are ye? Ye're no spies frae Brown & Root are ye?"

I bluffed. "I'm wi the Executive Team at Asco in Aberdeen."

"Asco? Here, is that nae whaur Jock Munro's at noo?"

"That's right. Jock's ane o wir bosses. This is Jock's car I'm driving."

"Ye'll be a'right, then. Jock's Volvo, right enaff! On ye go!"

With that he hoisted the barrier, waved us on and we drove ahead. Even before we could see any of the yard, or any of the work in progress, our eyes were opened by the sight of the road ahead. Here was a brand new carriageway stretching along the flat plain to a distant horizon. Although it was a clear day we could not make out where it ended. This was particularly astonishing as all over the North of Scotland we had to drive and survive on narrow twisting roads which, the authorities explained, was due to the rolling terrain and lack of funding for improvements. Here, in front of us, we viewed a highway, properly laid, kerbed and lined and perfectly flat. Miles of it.

Right! Open road, smooth surface, clear day, no traffic (or Traffic Cops), two litres, 98 octane fuel with added Redex, twin carburettors, seat belts fastened in the safest car in Europe. Foot to the floor. Let's see how much velocity is in this Volvo. And before any ecomentalists or Elf'n'Safety experts begin with their tut-tutting, I had the World's foremost expert on these matters sitting beside me in the passenger seat, egging me on. In no time at all we were up to the legal limit of 60MPH, admiring the stability of the steed as well as its unexpected urgency. By the time we had soared to 104 we had run out of daring and could finally see our target.

We slowed down and approached the imposing steel portals that marked the entrance to the construction complex. Beyond the gates we could see half-built fabrication sheds the size of aircraft hangars joined by wide concrete driveways stretching as far west as we had just driven.

There were only a few pieces of steel fabrications and no indication, as yet, of the leviathans that would be launched from this site over the next twenty-five years. It was, nevertheless, an impressive demonstration of how so much effective infrastructure can be assembled in a short time. All this within a year from conception and all built by private enterprise. This was a salutary lesson. Obviously the major operators and their contractors were better at oiling the wheels and getting things done than gormless governments, local and national. What Donald Trump would not give for that kind of co-operation! Thirty-five years later when most of the oil has been produced and the tax revenues spent, Ardersier has reverted to a caravan park and we still have to risk our lives travelling between the Oil Capital of Europe and The Capital of the Highlands on the intestinal A96. And I get a ticking off if I go above 50!

Wheels go round!

# 9. The North Sea Bubble Club

Mobility breeds ambition and ambition is driven by mobility. I'm sorry if that sounds too philosophical and out of place with the prevailing whimsy, but these sentiments are borne out not only by my personal observations and musings but by professional people whose working title ends in "ologist" and starts with "Anthrop" "Socio" and "Psycho" but, before you get bored and skip to Chapter 8, I will try and keep you hooked by informing you that this is a tale of a football match. OK, girls, you can turn the pages now.

Following the Influx of 1971, wherein I had become exposed to the cross-culture of returning Colonials and invading Europeans, and the frantic activity of 1972, during which I passed my driving test, acquired a Volvo and motored to exotic locations like Invergordon and Kilmarnock, my curious mind had been aroused by my own increasing mobility as well as by the giddying dislocation of my new colleagues, friends and clients. Everybody was adjusting to new sets of circumstances and adapting as well as possible to cope with increasing societal demands while trying to grasp the blossom of opportunity. It was in this time that I succumbed to the Deadly Sin of Ambition.

I do not think that Ambition is included in that Satanic Septet but I am pretty sure it must nestle somewhere beside Envy, Lust and Avarice and the other sins that drive the rest of our thrusting, grasping world but, hitherto, had not bothered me too much. Okay, Sloth and Gluttony had enjoyed my patronage at any given opportunity and they still do—but I am still alive. Although I have never been truly happy with all the striving, deprivation and self-flagellation that accompanies personal target setting there must have been something in my genetic or social make-up that allowed me to entertain thoughts about taking out an insurance policy,

121

buying my own house and looking for a better job, all of which I did during 1973.

Buying the insurance policy was probably a result of slick salesmanship on the part of the silver-tongued George Duffus, a friend of Alex Forbes from his connections in the entertainment industry. Along with Alex and Graeme Thomson I had been charged by Jim Simpson to attend a business dinner held in The Caledonian Hotel. He said it would be useful in our commercial and cultural development. In the light of our experience at the Citroen SM Launch debacle we should have been forewarned. The soiree was run by an association known as "Forty Round the Middle Club," and the Function Room at the Caledonian was filled mostly by plump, red-faced men with short haircuts, grey suits and shiny shoes, all laughing at their own jokes. Not my usual crowd. I guessed that the "Forty" referred to the average age of those attending but was informed by one of the jovial jesters that it referred to the minimum measurement of their waistbands. That fitted.

The evening proved to be duller than I expected. As a refreshing highlight, however, the cabaret act performed by George Duffus lifted the tedium and I was happy to tell him so when he came to join us after his forty minute set. George had honed his craft on the Folk Circuit following a similar path to Billy Connolly, Jasper Carrot and Mike Harding but not quite to the same acclaim or level of financial success. He had a genuine, easy wit and a calm, professional delivery. He had also done his homework and managed to include aphorisms about many of those attending in his routine.

Anyone who can write and deliver witty ditties about Insurance Companies, Quantity Surveyors, and Building Societies has to be worth his salt. Planning officials and bankers were much easier targets. George was also sufficiently pragmatic to remember that his "day-job" was selling insurance policies and he wasted little time with fripperies. While passing the port he casually enquired what kind of "cover" I had. Thinking that he had heard about my notorious clumsiness I imagined that he was alluding to some kind of napkin that would prevent any wine from being spilled on my Hepworth's three-piece suit. Without taking undue advantage of my naivety George went on to outline the benefits of having the necessary insurance, particularly if I had ambitions to join the property market. I was sold and I think he also mopped up commissions from Alex and Graeme who had similar ambitions. George was quite a salesman.

Alex had become besotted with his girlfriend, Linda, whistled through a whirlwind courtship, engagement and marriage and bought a flat at 438 Holburn Street. I learned from swapping notes on the progress of his acquisition that in addition to paying The Seller for your selected property you had to pay the Mortgage Lender for providing the lump sum, the Insurance Company for covering the risk of death and default on payments on that lump sum, The Solicitor for checking with others that the papers are in order for you to part with the same lump sum and the Surveyor for checking that the property will not crumble before the ink is dry on all the documents. All of this ensures that these honourable professionals earn their fees in order to be able to afford their high-priced properties in the West End and can indulge in evenings of self-congratulation such as we had with the Forty Round the Middle Club.

By good fortune, or rather, by being in a job with a regular income and by virtue of fine fellowship with some of my team-mates at my new football team—Hermes FC, I was in regular contact with budding professionals such as the brothers Fred and Les Dalgarno, plying their trade as conveyancing solicitors with Paull & Williamsons, who offered me friendly advice and steered me towards buying my own flat at 14 Watson Street. I had to forsake my place in the squad at the slightly higher placed Shamrock. This was due to a combination of events in that their greater footballing status demanded guaranteed availability on match-days (which conflicted with my new work schedule) as well as compulsory attendance at training on Thursdays (which interfered with my romantic aspirations). Although I have many fond memories of my many friends and the fun we had at Shamrock I had no option in 1972 but to move on and pay more attention to the increasing pressures of life and love.

The Volvo, which had proven such an unexpected bonus to my geographical mobility, a springboard to increasing my knowledge of the countryside, engendering my curiosity and awareness as well as being a boost to my personal status had gone, as Asco had traded it in against Jock Munro's new Range Rover (TST 9K.) As a fairly recent recruit to the driving fraternity I could not hold court with "real motorists" and compare notes on engine performance, handling characteristics, ride quality, stowage capabilities or any of the "Gizmos" with which petrolheads can hold sway in a barroom debate, but I knew from the first time I climbed *up* into Jock's imposing new vehicle that I was stepping into Automotive History.

This mustard coloured, aluminium bodied, geometric lump on chunky-tyred alloy-shod wheels, all four driven by a 3500cc Buick V8 and GM automatic box with an ergonomically designed interior, featuring waterproof lighting and seats clad in synthetic vinyl that could be cleaned by power-washer, might have been designed by Jock as ideal transport for driving across Dava Moor carrying a posse of hunters, their guns, ammunition and provisions and sufficient space in the rear to haul their "bag" back to the lodge.

Brits and Europeans were amazed by this automotive masterpiece, Americans less so. I recall a visit that we had to make up to Asco's new project at Peterhead. One of the Klondykers newly arrived from Louisiana was Allen Wagley, owner of a welding company that had enjoyed quite a bit of construction business in Alaska, who was aiming to replicate that success in the North Sea. He had been scouting for potential shorebase sites suitable for large-scale steel fabrication, and his slippery sales pitch had clearly impressed Jim Simpson sufficiently to warrant a consultation with Jock Munro and a guided tour of our putative development on South Bay. Eager to impress Wagley, Jim, a noted connoisseur of cars, suggested we take him in the brand new Range Rover

Nothing in Allen Wagley's earlier achievements or subsequent history indicated that he merited such VIP treatment, but Jim insisted that he was a key to Peterhead's future as a feeder site to Ardersier and Invergordon, and we were guided to treat him as another Mitch Watt or Elmer Adkins. Although I am not noted for assessing folks on first impressions I think I got this one right. Wagley was short in stature with weasel-like features, dressed in "Oil Trash" livery and spoke in a nasal monotone. He favoured derogatory comments over compliments and wasted little time with pleasantries or small talk. As we approached the Range Rover he uttered.

"You gotta van? Heck, it's only got two doors! Why'nt we take mah vee-hickul?"

"If you prefer."

Jock was nonplussed, wondering what could be more suitable than his brand new steed.

"Ah gotta rental car raht heah!"

We turned to gaze on Wagley's Wagon, a shiny new four door saloon in pearlescent purple, lots of chrome and glitter, humps and bumps with all the style and grace of a Codona's dodgem—a Ford Cortina Mark III. Jock and I looked at each other, silently agreeing on the comparative properties of the automobiles on offer and, I think, reaching consensus on a value judgment of our prospective client. The man talks more than he knows.

"I think we would be better in the 'van.' The road to Peterhead's pretty rough."

Jock's diplomacy had saved the day and we clambered into his Range Rover. By the time we had passed Newburgh on the coast road via Cruden Bay, Wagley had softened his truculent tone and conceded that Jock's "Vee-hickul" was a "neat ole Jeep."

There were hundreds of newcomers to the North east of Scotland from all parts of the globe. Sociologists and economists called this "inward mobility" rather than "immigration" which, thanks to Enoch Powell and others, had become recognised as a pejorative term. In addition to the influx from overseas there was an equal volume of inward mobility from other parts of the UK, as word spread that Aberdeen was no longer a backwater with a cold granite façade but was now "Boom Town" with real jobs paying above average wages and offering prospects of stardom.

Quite a lot of nonsense was spouted in the Media about the expatriates' exploits and I would not wish to add to any of that for fear of authenticating such hyperbole, but there was an appreciable increase in job opportunities and the salaries offered were well ahead of the national average. The hierarchical control of the leading local industrial, commercial and professional employers (mostly family-owned and run) that had stifled mobility and ambition in our region for centuries had been rendered impractical by the "Oil Boom."

As Regent Road had been at the centre of this maelstrom from the earliest days, as the temporary home for incoming explorers, and I was one of very few available locals it was unsurprising that, even with no formal qualifications and only limited experience, I would be offered a variety of exciting job openings and I have to admit my head was turned by a few.

A combination of loyalty to Jim and Maggie Simpson and scepticism of the long-term prospects of some of those offering "new lamps for old," kept me grounded. Although I was no "job-hopper," I was well enough aware of my capabilities to know that I could pick up a well-paying number if I wanted or if I had to. By 1973 most of the early tenants, Amoco, BP, Conoco and Sedco, had moved on to grand new purpose-built premises on the expanding industrial estates at Dyce and Tullos, and I spent more of my time travelling to and from those sites.

On a social level too the local catering and entertainment business had exploded like one of those "fairy rings" you see on manicured lawns. From a paucity of pubs and a dearth of dining establishments, Aberdeen had become almost cosmopolitan, acquiring a few more Chinese and Indian outlets, as well as an Italian Trattoria (Luigi's) and an upmarket French Restaurant (Gerard's.) All the city hotels were filled and some of the more attractive country residences were able to open outside the tourist season (August.)

Wednesday nights at the Palace Ballroom was a case in point. These had been an innovation in the mid-sixties by the owners, Rank Organisation, aimed at the more mature clientele (twenty-five-plus) offering dining, dancing, live music and late-licence drinking. Demographic studies had determined that, throughout Britain, there was increasing prosperity, with higher disposable incomes among the junior executive brigade, who were seeking out more sophisticated mid-week entertainment. Candle-lit dining tables served with bar suppers and a selection of fine wines, had filled the Locarnos and Roxys throughout the land and generated riches for Rank.

In depressed Aberdeen, however, with no discernible executive population, the Wednesdays at The Palace did not thrive as in Manchester or Birmingham but evolved (or degenerated) into "Grab-a-Granny" Disco nights where the few punters with ready cash in mid-week comprised a disparate collection of divorcees looking for new chances to fail, returning Servicemen looking for some sort of loyalty reward, commercial salesmen with overstretched expense accounts and the occasional footballer looking for a sneaky result away from home (until spotted by the eagle-eyed Eddie Turnbull.)

These were fairly desperate affairs and the cocktail of testosterone and alcohol led to many an altercation. The frisson of excitement was heightened by the influx of foreign males with their easy familiarity and much higher levels of disposable income. The Aberdeen Ladies suddenly had a new framework of opportunities. Some noses were definitely put out of joint.

As a service company and in the long tradition of Scottish hospitality, we had tried as much as we could to make all newcomers welcome in their new home. I hope I have adequately described how happily everyone seemed to have settled into the Regent Road site and how a genuine *esprit de corps* had developed almost organically. With growing successes, however, each company was spreading upwards and outwards to bigger and better facilities on

127

the edge of town and corporate centrism was replacing communal collectivism.

There was no prospect of repeating the Barytes Cutters Ball. Each growing organisation had enough to attend to with their own staff and customers with less inclination to include outsiders in their festivities. Some will contend that "Big Oil" cannot or will not engender any form of community spirit, but I will testify that we did have something approaching that in Aberdeen in 1973 and we tried to foster that and keep it going. This was our City, our Industry and we wanted both to survive and thrive.

Beyond the pubs and parties there was a real scarcity of entertainment for our incoming friends. Two dilapidated theatres, an ill-equipped music hall, forty fading flick-joints rapidly being converted to bingo halls and bowling alleys, did not represent Xanadu in the cultural desert of the North East of Scotland. Those with deeper pockets moved towards establishing the North Sea Petroleum Club. That was clearly aimed at high rollers and well beyond the aspirations of those without a forgiving expenses account.

My own tastes and interests have always been simple and unsophisticated but I like to think that I have usually been willing to join in where others are having healthy sport and harmless fun. Whenever there was an opportunity for a game of football I would be a ready participant. Bobby Livingston, a star striker with Montrose FC and a sales representative with Olivetti, was usually the instigator of such opportunities. With his pleasant manner Bobby could gain access to many offices in his attempt to sell typewriters and he would be a regular visitor at Regent Road. After the predictable preamble, the conversation would turn to his main interest of football and, even though he was a part-time professional, he would always be up for organising a "bounce game" wherever he could find a suitable venue and sufficient players.

Those with boots and transport would find themselves roped in to play a variety of venues from Cowie Park, Stonehaven to Kingseat Mental Hospital to be pitched into teams comprising some of Bobby's fellow professionals like Dennis D'Arcy, Doug Gallacher and Bryan Thomson alongside amateur hopefuls such as Bill Bavidge, Lenny Nicol and Donald Jamieson. In the course of these keenly contested outings we would come across some newcomers that Bobby had trawled in from his calls at all the other new offices.

Helge Sorheim had arrived recently as a trainee with Smedvig. He showed a decent turn of speed and a bit of Continental flair. Clive Riddell was a Shipping Clerk with Offshore Marine and had come up from Yarmouth. Clive was a stuffy Right Back and reputedly had trials with Norwich City. Paul McHugh too had trials with Norwich. Paul was an Aberdeen boy whose family had decamped to Great Yarmouth in pursuit of the "Gas Boom" and had followed the chase back home. He played with us at Hermes where he displayed fantastic ball control and dribbling skills but showed little appetite for what is now termed as "putting in a shift" which probably explains why he was selling ball bearings rather than continuing his football career.

I cannot remember exactly how it came about but, as a result of these casual football gatherings, some of us took to thinking that we should try to organise other sporting events and involve more of the other new faces. One of the key drivers was Dave Craig. Dave was a suave, smooth-talking rep with Onshore Communications, selling new-fangled pagers to the growing ranks of high-pressure oil executives who had to be contactable outside office hours. He was a permanent fixture in the oilfield's favourite watering hole, The Marcliffe, and would join us while satisfying our thirst after those evening efforts. Although he claimed to have once played for Kilmarnock he never joined any of our bounce games, citing the usual excuses of pressure of business and, the clincher, a "bad knee." As a keen "networker," Dave was obviously interested in spreading his contacts and suggested the use of his offices and networks to explore and exploit the idea. He worked with an old schoolmate of mine, Donald Blair, who was not in the least bit sporting but equally keen on developing social and business links.

After a couple of pints or three we all agreed this sounded an attractive proposition and convened a meeting at their offices in the Ariel Complex at Abbotswell.

Everyone who has ever been at meetings with me knows that I have an abundant distaste for the formalities and the inevitable obfuscation associated with such events, and as the mass of male bodies crammed into Donald Blair's tiny office on a fine summer evening I gravitated towards the easiest exit door. Alex Forbes and the Dalgarno brothers felt much more comfortable in these circumstances, settling somewhere in the middle and handling the brouhaha with ease. All sorts of suggestions and proposals were flying about as I leant on the door-jamb and yawned. We discussed rugby matches, golf tournaments, swimming galas, regattas, skiing trips and go-karting Grand Prix, all of which floundered either on the lack of numbers or available funds.

After about two hours of stating the bleedin' obvious (par for the course in meetings,) we arrived at a concrete proposal of forming a football team. Graham Fox of Occidental felt he could raise the sponsorship to fund a team strip. Alex thought that Asco would stretch to buying a ball or two and Ian Maitland reckoned he could negotiate a deal for providing bus transport to some of the mooted long distance matches. By the end of the evening we were talking about playing against teams all over Scotland. Some even suggested matches against a Great Yarmouth Select and the sillier section got on to the possibility of touring Holland and Norway. My sole contribution was to conjure up the name for this fledgling organisation.

Scepticism about the longevity of the oil business in Aberdeen was still prevalent in my thinking. Some of the exaggerated stories in the media, and wild conjecture among some of my peers, led me to consider comparable historical episodes of hyperbolic speculation, so when we got round to selecting a name for our group, I proffered "The North Sea Bubble Club." As many in the assembly had never heard of "The South Sea Bubble," to which I was alluding, I received a few of those "What the hell is he talking about?" looks. Over many years in this business I have become inured to such stupefied stares, as cultural education and historical allegory remain the preserve of surprisingly few, and I had to rely on the knowledge and wisdom of Les Dalgarno to explain the source and relevance of the title.

Nobody else came up with a suitable alternative and my idea was accepted, but the momentum of the meeting dictated that we had to mull it over for another half an hour or so; we ended up with the full working title of "The North Sea Bubble Sporting Club," although from thenceforth, in any conversation relating to our activities nobody used anything more extensive than the accepted moniker of "The Bubble Club." Graham Fox was good for his promise of a set of jerseys, shorts and socks although everyone suspected that one of Occidental's eager suppliers had come up with the sixty-five quid necessary to buy the kit.

I was there to witness Alex Forbes managing to wheedle £30 out of a reluctant Mr. Fraser, Asco's Chief Accountant, recently appointed by our new masters (Sidlaw Industries,) to buy some Mitre "T" Panel Footballs. This achievement alone was enough to secure Alex's place in the team. Ask anyone who ever managed to get anything beyond a grunt out of Mr. Fraser and you will appreciate the significance.

My memory of our few fixtures is fairly vague and I cannot recall the name of the opposition we faced but I remember that we enjoyed a close victory in Inverness and had celebrated with a few ales before convening in the local Chinese restaurant. We then had to make a quick exit as Graham Fox strained Occidental-Oriental relations with his Pythonesque interpretation of the Menu. We hurried happy but hungry pursued by Hong Kong Fuey with a livid expression, swearing incomprehensibly and wielding a mighty cleaver. Ian Maitland had fulfilled his offer of a good deal on the provision of transport, however the driver of the dilapidated bus that we had on this jaunt to Inverness was glad that his passengers were young and fit enough to give it a shove when its expired battery caused it to fail and we had to push-start it and get us back to Aberdeen. The chipper in Nairn was glad to see us.

Flushed with success and fostering a fair deal of camaraderie we started talking about more exotic and exciting fixtures. Dave Craig, who still had not donned the goalie's jersey but was always on the periphery and inevitably in the Marcliffe, came up with the idea of inviting a team of "All-Stars" comprising retired professionals that had been enjoying a bit of publicity and raising some funds for charitable causes. He thought that a match with the Bubble Club against some of the most famous names in Scottish Football would be a sure-fire money-spinner as well as a decent sporting challenge.

When we quizzed him about some of the "Names" involved with these "All-Stars" Dave quoted some of his old colleagues at Kilmarnock who were familiar only to those with cigarette card collections of faded footballers. Detecting our cynicism he then pitched in some real notables such as Bobby Shearer, the former Rangers Skipper, Billy McNeill and Bertie Auld, the Celtic Legends. He had our attention from that point and as he casually dropped into his delivery that the one and only Jim Baxter was an occasional participant we were sold. When can they come? Where can we play? Will we get in the papers? How about TV coverage?

Following the initial hysteria I have to admit there was the usual scepticism and inevitable dismissal of the idea. The Bubble Club would be no match for any decent amateur side never mind a team of pros, no matter how old and fat they had become. We could barely scrape together the resources to kit out a scratch eleven and play a few bounce games.

There was nowhere to stage an event that would need to draw a gate of thousands to cover the basic expenses. Dave Craig was all mouth and flared trousers. He couldn't deliver. Could he?

I must relent on my own scepticism about committees in general and the Bubble Club in particular for, in spite of all the doubters, we did manage to persuade the "All Stars" to venture outside the Central Belt for the first time and come to visit the Granite City. All we had to do was to put out a team, find a venue and provide overnight accommodation for about twenty players and officials. We had a month or so to plan the event and, as the match was scheduled for early August, before the regular football season begun, we managed to secure the Linksfield Stadium. Hotel accommodation in Aberdeen was at a premium but, on weekends, there was easier availability and we managed to block-book the George Hotel for the Saturday night. The George had always been a bit of a favourite with visiting sides and it had a brand new Disco Bar. All we needed now was a team that would provide meaningful opposition to this incoming team of Superstars.

The mood was high and there was a new edge to our practise games. We now had real competition for places in the side as better players imagined the prospect of pitting their wits and matching their skills against their heroes. Bobby Livingston, Dennis D'Arcy, Doug Gallacher and the other semi-pro footballers in the oilfield circle were itching to be part of this great event. Sponsorship had been facilitated by the prospect of all the big names and we easily covered the costs of hiring the stadium and the hotel with a little extra for an "entertainment fund."

As the day approached there were a few pitfalls and some disappointments. Our semi-professional "ringers" all had to withdraw as the Scottish Football Association and their part-time employers' insurance policies would not cover their appearance in "unofficial" friendly matches. Dave Craig did finally don the goalie's jersey for a practice match but pulled a muscle in the warm-up so we never did find out whether he was any good between the sticks. He found a plausible substitute in the form of Johnny Low, one-time goalkeeper with Fraserburgh, but long retired and beyond the control of the SFA. I had my own letdown as I found out that I was excluded from the starting eleven. Whilst not wishing to appear immodest I felt that I had been one of the better players in our regular squad, but I had to bow to the consensus that, as a charitable organisation, The Bubble Club had to favour those who had put in the effort off the pitch rather than on it.

Those who had done most to generate sponsorship had to get

their rewards so Graham, Alex, Les and Fred all had a starting spot in their favoured positions. Ian used his bus pass to secure his place on the right wing. There was a feeling that we should try to emphasise our international connections so Norwegian Helge Sorheim and "The Flying Dutchman" Huub van Vlerken were included. Clive and Paul got in on the strength of their trials at Norwich. Ronnie Graver had actually played for Norwich but was well aware of his lack of fitness and declined the opportunity to play. He was happy to take the role as Team Coach. Bill Bavidge completed the starting XI.

There were regrets too in the opposition camp. None of the superstars from the Celtic faction would be coming and the only name that we recognised as being close to fame and stardom was Johnny Divers. There was a better representation from the Rangers side and we were pleased to hear that the legendary Johnny Hubbard would be making a rare appearance. Some of the more cynical amongst us suggested that listing the pre-match venue as "The Lodge," the newly refurbished Disco Bar in the George Hotel, might have appeared off-putting to those of a Celtic persuasion but more welcoming and familiar to those with Orange connections.

One of our devious ploys at making the match competitive and avoiding the likelihood of the Bubble Club suffering an embarrassing tanking was to use the bulk of our "entertainment" fund to fill our guests full of beer on the Saturday night in order to slow them down on the Sunday. Our scheming came to nought, however, as we met up with "The All Stars" at the Lodge to discover that many of them would take only soft drinks, and those that could be tempted were sufficiently seasoned to withstand any effects of the demon drink.

There was a major blow with the announcement that Jim Baxter would not be coming to the party or to the game. This was crushing for those of us who had revered "Slim Jim" in his heyday and had relished the prospect of merely being on the same pitch as one of Scotland's genuine World Class players. We had sold a lot of tickets and secured a decent amount of sponsorship based on

Baxter's promised presence.

Our guests offered genuine apologies but were not surprised by the great man's non-appearance. His notoriety was not, apparently, misplaced and he was becoming increasingly unreliable. In compensation they thought that Jim's "no-show" would be easier on our "Entertainment Fund" and leave more to contribute to their Charities. We might also stand a better chance of getting a kick at the ball during the game.

The match itself was fairly lacklustre. The Bubble Club players were mostly twenty-something, fit and eager. The All-Stars, mainly in their late thirties and forties and slowed by the multiple injuries that are the lot of Scottish footballers, could still display the skill and control that ensured that the ball did the work, causing us youngsters to run about aimlessly.

They coasted to a two-nil lead by half-time, including a classic penalty goal from Johnny Hubbard. I had read in the *Weekly News* (Scotland's authoritative journal on all football matters and almost trustworthy) that, in his long career with Rangers, Hubbard always picked the same spot to shoot from and would hit a crisp side-footer with his right foot to the goalkeeper's left scoring with sixty-five out of sixty-eight efforts. I assumed that our goalie would have known this and might have had a stab at grabbing some glory by being one of the few to save a Hubbard spot-kick. Johnny H. calmly slotted the ball in his usual spot as Johnny L dived half-heartedly to his right. Goal!

While our guests congratulated their scorer and shuffled back to the halfway line for the restart our team watched as Johnny Low, expressionless, pulled himself slowly to his feet, dusted himself down, reached down into his kit-bag tucked neatly inside his right hand post, pulled out a half-bottle of vodka, took a healthy slug, opened a packet of fags, lit one up and had a few puffs. He did not even bother to pick the ball out of the net, leaving that to Alex Forbes. Ronnie Graver was livid and turned to me on the sidelines, scowling.

"Right, John, get stripped. You're going on second half."

I was dumbstruck. Although still excited by the prospect of pitching up against the pros I did not much fancy going between the sticks. My goalkeeping ability could be termed as only fair and I feared we were facing an inevitable onslaught as our guests started to overpower our flagging defence. Dave Craig came to my rescue and volunteered to don the gloves. Helge came in for the break complaining of a calf-strain and I was happy to take his place on the left wing.

My pleasure at gaining a place was tempered by the prospect of facing Bobby Shearer, a fearsome competitor with a penchant for kicking lumps out of many an outside-left. He had seemed an amiable sort of cove when we had chatted the previous night in the pub and was almost gentlemanly in our early encounters. It was only after I had flicked the ball over his head, raced by him and tried a shot on goal that skimmed the crossbar that I could gauge his reputation.

"Nice try, big man," he muttered as I tracked back to face the goal kick, "Ye widnae have got away wi' that ten years ago, I would've cleaved ye in two."

I believed him. I had seen him play. To our relief the All-Stars eased up in the latter stages of the game and somehow, probably charitably, we carved out a 2-2 draw. We shook hands, showered and retired to the Lodge for a few more beers and a bit of supper.

Amid the bonhomie and the backslapping there were the usual courteous thank-you messages, friendly threats and promises of a re-match with vague ideas for further contests but, as time passed and the North Sea continued its mushrooming growth, there was no repeat of this event. Some might mourn the passing of another example of fading community spirit or despise the rising corporatism that would provide bigger, better-funded occasions over the next thirty years but we must concede that the forces of Global Economics are mightier even than Scottish sentiments for self-sufficiency.

You might wonder how a charity football match had anything to do with mobility and ambition, so I should explain. Without the availability of a company car I would not have been able to join in Bobby's bounce games and would probably have been restricted to playing only in Hermes' Amateur League fixtures. Without this added mobility I would not have been exposed to the wider mix of people from other parts of the UK and Europe. From these additional contacts my mind was opened to different views and higher aspirations. I never enjoyed anything more than schoolboy dreams in my ambitions as a footballer. Of course I imagined myself scoring the winning goal for Scotland in the Home International at Wembley, but I was now twenty-five and realism had begun to dig its claws into my daydreaming. Nevertheless, here I was playing against Bobby Shearer, who had played for Scotland at Wembley, albeit in the most disastrous rout in Scottish Football history, when we lost 9-3 to the "Auld Enemy."

The real ambitions that were being planted were in working terms. Most of the guys that I played with in the Bubble Club were doing similar jobs in shipping, forwarding, materials handling, transport and storage with other service companies within our expanding industry.

There was increasing talk of fantastic new openings at home and overseas, offering unheard of salaries and benefits. Until this time very few of my fellow Aberdonians had displayed any belief or ambitions in the North Sea adventure; however, from about this time onward, attitudes, including my own, started to change.

# 10. Onwards and Upwards Part I

As much as passing my driving test and gaining access to company wheels had allowed me to open my eyes and raise my levels of ambition, I still could not qualify as "well travelled." Apart from a single jaunt in 1968 with ten mates, in a Leyland J2 Minibus along the Hippy Trail to Marrakesh, I had not been abroad, never been on a package holiday, not even flown in an aeroplane. At University I would listen to fellow students regale me with tales of their exploits in exotic Egypt or the joys of sun, sea, sand (and the other) in the Greek Islands and these would feed my wanderlust. Meeting incomers arriving from all parts of the globe merely exacerbated my sense of envy and emphasised my need to get up and go and start travelling.

Imagine my excitement when Kenny Mann, the Amoco Materials Supervisor, came to us with the chance of a helicopter flight. Wow! My first airborne opportunity—in a chopper! Bristow had offered a free flight, which was a major consideration, given that they normally charged £1500 per flying hour. Imagine the bragging rights in the pub, swapping stories with my buddies about recent escapades. This would beat any tale of a day trip to Dieppe or a week in Majorca—a private flight in a charter helicopter; do you know how much that costs?

There was a slight snag, however, as Kenny went on to explain. In order to satisfy their Board of Trade Licence, Bristow Helicopters had to conduct periodic test flights and also had to prove, once and for all, that the Sikorsky S61 aircraft could settle and re-launch from a landing in water. This was no problem. One look at the craft reveals that, with its tub shaped fuselage, it was designed for floating as well as flying. The slight element of danger, which never entered my eager young head at the time, was that they required real people to be on board the helicopter during the test. From what

139

I have learned since, and have experienced first hand during the underwater rotation test that comprised part of my later survival training, volunteering to travel by chopper and land on a stretch of water, even one as accessible and relatively calm like the Loch of Skene, is not a wise move and, in light of the many incidents involving helicopters over the years, is something that would not be allowed by any self-respecting risk assessor, Board of Trade or otherwise. Water take-offs and landings are strictly for the birds.

Totally oblivious to the risks and caring only for the adventure in hand, we rolled up at Bristow's hangar in Dyce heliport at 0600 on a cold crisp, spring morning. Alex, Graeme, Kenny, Jimmy, two technicians and yours truly piled into the commodious cabin of the S61, listened intently to the safety briefing, donned our ear defenders, tied the lifejackets around our waists above our street clothing (survival suits had not yet been introduced) and prepared for take-off. Nerves and blood pressure increased at approximately the same rate as the accelerating rotor blades, but our soaring anxiety and lofty ambitions were met only with anticlimax.

Over the Tannoy the pilot uttered an apology and announced that the test would have to be cancelled. While warming up from a sub-zero outdoor temperature a part of the windscreen had cracked, rendering the aircraft as less than airworthy. He went on to explain that an immediate repair was impossible and that it would be at least another week before the fault could be rectified and the helicopter returned to service. Bristow would have to reschedule the test. It was a major disappointment to all of us but still a tale worthy of a couple of renditions in subsequent pub exchanges. Do you know how much a windscreen for a Sikorsky S61 costs?

Kenny recognised our disappointment and was most conciliatory, promising that he would do his best to try and arrange another chance for a chopper ride. True to his word, he did fix things and, in due course, we all managed to hitch a lift on one of the occasional charters that came up over the next year or so. Jimmy Gallan, rightfully, was awarded the first opportunity and jumped at his invitation when a diamond drill bit was ordered for urgent despatch out to the *Sedco 135F* rig at short notice. Of course, Jimmy took the drill bit with him in the back of his estate car and probably helped load it on to the helicopter and off at the other end.

We were all agog as we met him on his return later that same day and badgered him with a barrage of inane questions on his experience and his observations.

"How big is it?"

"Did it catch fire?"

"How fierce are the waves?"

"Did you get a T-Bone Steak?"

Jimmy had obviously relished his trip and had the look of a young boy returning from a visit to Santa's Grotto, but regretted he had not had sufficient time to feast his eyes on all the wondrous machinery at his disposal. He thanked Kenny for giving him the chance to achieve one of the dreams that he had nurtured since starting in this business over five years before. He had met our good friend William J Hirondelle, ("Running Bear") the Amoco Drilling Superintendent, who had given him a guided tour of the rig. Meeting Elmer Adkins, the rig manager, on his return, he also thanked him for the hospitality given to him on board the *135F* but, typically, gave a tongue-in-cheek riposte as Elmer chided him whether he had done "his day's work out there."

"Hemmin, Elmer, I thocht ye telt me they workit hard on yer rig!"

"Whaddya mean, Jimmy?"

"I nivver seen a one o them dae a hand's turn a the time I was oot there."

"Well, Jim, that's on account of you being late with the bit. You'll need to sharpen up!"

Elmer and Jimmy had a mutual regard for each other's capabilities and this was reinforced by their easy banter. I am sure that Jimmy would have loved to try his hand at the drilling game and, with his undoubted ability with machinery and commendable man-management skills, would have been a sure-fire success.

141

Elmer recognised Jimmy's worth and could easily have persuaded him to join up if it were not for the "Gentlemen's Agreement," between Jim Simpson and his key clients, relating to not poaching each others' staff.

This agreement was called into question, however, later that year when Kenny Mann was persuaded to swim against the tide and become Asco's General Manager. Pat Morrison, our secretary and receptionist moved to ODS and Hebbie Spence, our mechanic went to join IMC.

Rules are obviously meant to be broken, as I was to find out to my own surprise a little later on, but nobody was going to be allowed to entice Jimmy Gallan from his key position. Jim Simpson had a full appreciation of his assets.

The opportunity for my debut flight arrived later in 1972 as the *Sedco 135F* contract was being transferred from Amoco to Conoco. A special flight had been arranged to cover the delivery of some fancy new satellite navigation items for the "spud-in" of Conoco's second well and, on the same trip, return some valuable pieces of kit that Amoco had on rental for the well just completed. Kenny must have alerted Bill Byatt, the Conoco Materials Supervisor, of his promise to arrange helicopter trips for those disappointed by the aborted trial run and the ever-obliging Bill delivered on the deal with his customary grace and good humour.

"Young John, I need a helper, are you available?"

"Nae bother, Bill. What do you need?"

"I have to go out to the rig and conduct an inventory for the change-over and I need an independent witness for the auditors. You'll do. How are you fixed for tomorrow?"

"Who cares? For a free flight I'll be your independent thingummy. What time?"

"Seven o'clock sharp at Bristow's. Bring a pad and pencil."

Although I have always been notoriously unresponsive in the mornings I was up at the crack of dawn, which in an Aberdeen summer means about three in the morning; I had hardly slept a wink that night as I was hell-bent on making this appointment. In the event I could have slept until ten as a seasonal mist delayed the departure and Bill and I were forced to linger about the heliport for several precious hours. No matter, we eventually took off and, after the early discomfort and disorientation associated with one's virgin flight, I began to appreciate the fantastic sensation of hovering above the earth and speeding at 120 knots out over the ploughed fields, the coastal dunes and onward to our destination in the grey North Sea approximately 150 miles away, midway between Scotland and Norway.

Naturally I was nervous. I had no preconception of the noise, vibration and swaying motion of the chopper, how cold it could be at an altitude of 2000 feet and how tiny everything appeared from that height. Although there was rarely anything in sight I gawped out through the misted window, eager for a sight of anything other than waves and seagulls and, after an hour and a bit I caught glimpse of the rig. In fact, the first thing I spotted as we descended to landing altitude was the supply boat, the *Smit Lloyd 103*. This was a vessel I had seen many times before as we had loaded it with mud, casing, drill pipe and containers of consumables and had held it in wonder as it stood proud of all the other puny fishing vessels in the overcrowded environment of Aberdeen Harbour. Now, from a vantage point of a couple of hundred of feet the *SL 103* resembled one of those model ships I had admired so often as a child seeing them being picked up and launched by their careful owners in the Duthie Park boating pond and now it just looked kinda cute. As I had seen photographs with the *SL103* alongside the rig in various locations, it was only when the form of the rig hove into view that I could gain any sort of perspective.

As the chopper descended towards the helipad on the easily recognisable tripod structure, I was astonished at the vision that I beheld. Although the supply boat resembled a boat-pond model, the *Sedco 135F* represented a true leviathan. While the shape was not unfamiliar I was unprepared for the overwhelming scale of the monster. It was as if someone had taken three sections of the Forth Bridge, Scotland's foremost engineering construction, formed them

143

into a triangle, and floated them out to the middle of the ocean. I noticed the Amoco decals on the windwall surrounding the drill floor.

These must have been the same massive structures I remembered filling two articulated lorries, requiring a "Wide Load" police escort when, earlier that year, we had hauled them from Lisco's factory in Whitemyres to Pocra Quay and loaded them onboard the *SL103*. They now looked like no bigger than the stickers you might have balanced gingerly on the point of your finger before dabbing them on to your latest Airfix model. It was phenomenal to behold back then and ranks, in my sense of wonder, with my first sightings of Mont Blanc or the Grand Canyon. I would have liked to compare it with the Eiffel Tower but, as it was foggy on the one day that I visited Paris, I missed that sight.

Landing on the rig felt a bit squidgy as, I have since learned, all helicopter touchdowns are, and I was glad to disembark and regain stability. A bit of a swell had built up on the sea and the waves were beginning to crest. This added to the seascape and to the adventure but killed the prospect of observing any interesting onboard activity as, having completed the well, the rig had been delayed in recovering the wellhead and moving on to the next location. In agreement with the fishermen the United Kingdom Offshore Operators Association (UKOOA) had undertaken that no hardware that might damage trawl nets would be left on the seabed. As a consequence a lot of time, effort and money has been expended over the years in cutting, releasing and recovering the heavy, intricate equipment that comprises a wellhead assembly.

Bill Byatt guided me to the Operator's office where he dutifully explained why we had come. He need not have bothered, as everyone knew the purpose of our visit, but we understood that Bill was just being his usual polite self and let him carry on regardless. Jack Ford was the Company Man, an absolute legend in the industry, held in the highest regard by oil explorers worldwide as an authority in offshore drilling. He was the leading member in the partnership of North Sea Drilling Consultants Ltd. The other partner was "Running Bear" and, between the two of them, they did more than most in those early days in our region in establishing the reputation of the offshore fraternity as hard working, high earning, high-living hedonists.

While onshore they reserved a suite at the Treetops Hotel, but did not always sleep there, had a chauffeur-driven limousine on twenty-four hour call, as they would rarely, if ever, be fit to drive themselves, and employed a full time PR agent, Kris Petersen, a stunning six foot brunette, reputedly a former Miss Denmark, who steered them to business meetings as well as arranging social engagements. There were stories about Jack and Running Bear being ferried from late-night parties, poured on to the helicopter and flown to the rig to fulfil their obligations as drilling consultants at the incredible rate of $500 per day. As I cannot testify that I was ever witness to such events, I can only report them as hearsay, but I did hear their employers verify that they were the best in the world at devising drill string combinations and directing downhole operations to their complete satisfaction. What else does anyone need to do to maintain a reputation?

The audit that had necessitated our trip offshore was very easily completed. All that Bill and I had to do was count some pallets of mud, a few surplus drill bits, tally the leftover casing pipe and take Jack Ford's word for whatever remained in the wellbore. All of this took us less than an hour. It is little wonder that our offshore counterparts have such a low opinion of the efforts of their shorebase servants. They should see how tough it is back at the office.

As we had an hour or so to fill in I had a chance to have a look around. There was no drilling or loading activity so there was little risk of getting in the way of anything dangerous. I saw a few faces that I recognised and with not much to do some of them were glad of someone to talk to and happily pointed out the various pieces of equipment that attracted my curiosity. Although I am the first to acknowledge a lack of a mechanical aptitude and would concede that my initial attempts at working with any new equipment usually

145

ends up with twisted thumbs or broken bits of valuable kit, I have always had a fascination with how things are made, where they are made and who makes them and it was an education to wander about the pump room, engine room and switchgear room, spotting the various pieces of machinery that I had only just heard of or read about.

I met up again with Pat Devery, recently promoted from Watchstander to Barge Engineer, who ably demonstrated the network of buttons, switches, knobs and gauges employed to control the tanks and valves of the ballasting operations of this sea monster. Fascinating!

There was, however, a trace of despondency in some of my conversations, even with those I had seen as cheery individuals, admittedly in a more more sociable surroundings like the Star & Garter. These were men who obviously enjoyed their work and would not swap their positions for anything onshore but, still, their comments tended towards pessimism. I realise now, of course, that this was my virgin visit, my first flight and I was enthralled at having landed in a wonderland beyond my wildest imagination.

To many of the guys on the rig this was their long-established workplace and they had long since gotten over the thrill of travelling for hours in a "flying fridge" to land on a hard metal hulk in the desolate North Sea with the prospect of spending long, boring days and long, lonely nights, interspersed by spells of feverish activity throwing big chunks of steel pipe into a hole in the ground, or pouring huge lengths of enormous anchor chain somewhere out of sight in the murky depths below. The *Sedco 135F* might have been one of the wonders of the modern world of technological progress but it was not anyone's idea of Shangri La.

Tedium is a main cause of despair in the offshore environment and I have noticed over the years that everyone, from roustabout to toolpusher, is usually much more enthusiastic and higher spirited when there is a demanding task at hand. Drill crews perk up when they face the prospect of running several thousand feet of drill pipe in and out of the hole. Marine hands are appreciably sharper when anchor handling or boat loading is under way and there is nothing more attractive to a mechanic than a major engine overhaul.

In between such golden moments there is an awful lot of standing and waiting and it takes a great deal of management skill in maintaining morale to ensure that people stay alert and aware in order that these very demanding tasks are conducted in a safe and efficient manner. Much has been written and recorded on the heroic adventures and the dramatic exploits of our Offshore Tigers but very little has been noted about the mundane routines and the boredom associated with their lives. Out of sight out of mind seems be the maxim. They get well paid for their troubles.

One of the palliatives used to ease the pain of working offshore, at least in the early days, was the food service and, before I had visited a rig, I had been persuaded by the many stories of roustabouts and roughnecks enjoying all-day dining, living high on the hog, with lashings of the best of ingredients and all for free. It was with high expectation, therefore, that I entered the galley, after Bill had suggested we go for something to eat before our flight back to town. It was five o'clock with the chopper due back at a little after six.

We were the first diners and we had the pick of the tables as well as first call on the menu but my first impressions did not meet with my extraordinarily high expectations. The galley was, of course, in the living quarters, at the "sharp" end of the rig, (if there can be such a thing on a triangular rig;) anyway, it was as far away from the dangerous part of the vessel, which was the derrick, the drill floor and the rest of the bits that would be set alight in the event of a "blow-out" from the wellbore. The room was a strange rhomboid shape as most of the accommodation had to be in order to fit in the confines of the structure.

The décor was extremely plain with tables designed for form and function rather than fashion. With the slight sea motion I could understand the need for having them bolted to the floor. The Formica surfaces and vinyl covered seating had also been designed for durability and ease of cleaning rather than creature comfort but I thought they might have been a bit more adventurous with the colour scheme. Red and white was perfectly all right for the outside of the rig but unacceptably bright under the fluorescent lights and a bit stark for indoors. The cutlery and tableware was suitably heavy duty, matching the clientele and the surroundings.

I felt pretty safe in these surroundings and fairly hungry too, as I had taken little more than orange juice and coffee to sustain me since breakfast, in fact that had been my breakfast. Okay, I was ravenous and eagerly anticipating a massive plate of chow. I had swallowed the hype and I was now prepared to swallow all the comestibles that this floating palace of epicurean delights could muster but was slightly disappointed to read on the hand-chalked board that tonight's offering was Chicken and Rice, Liver and Bacon or Mince 'n Tatties. I could get that at home!

As we were the only ones in the self-service queue and never having suffered from the British fear of raising complaints in eating establishments I queried what had become of the steaks, chops, lobsters, lasagne and other exotica that the articles in the papers had led me to expect. The steward was a Scouser, just like about every other steward I came across over the next twenty years of visiting offshore galleys. Why is that? He seemed like a pleasant enough chap and he offered the explanation that they had tried all the "fancy food" but affirmed:

"You Jocks just like yer mince and tatties an' a bit of haggis now and then. Don't yer?"

I helped myself to a bit of each (just for the purposes of sampling and reporting, you understand) and was unsurprised by the results. The presentation in a row of NAAFI style trays was none too appetising and it tasted no better than standard transport café fare. This eating-house would have represented little threat to Ida's on Market Street or Mary's Café on Waterloo Quay. As some of the crew drifted in I sought their opinions on the catering. There were no complaints about the size of the servings or the cleanliness and aside from the usual moans about the predictability of the menus and a demand for "chips with everything" there seemed to be a consensus that it was an acceptable standard. Some even motioned a word or two of praise for the special efforts that the caterers would make in preparing cakes for birthdays and such along with a surprising commendation for their presentation of the Cold Table on Sundays (when they had to shut down and clean the hot ovens and griddles). T-bone steaks were available and much appreciated but usually reserved for Saturdays or special occasions like Christmas or Easter or when VIPs came to call. Bill and I obviously did not come into that category.

We tidied up our dishes, said our thanks and returned to the office to check in for the return flight. The weather had abated and the office chatter was focussed on resuming the task of launching the divers, setting explosives, blasting the wellhead and recovering the debris before setting off on tow for the new location. It sounds exciting as I write it out even after thirty-five years, but all these demanding and sometimes dangerous activities are invariably planned and conducted on board a rig in a deadpan, almost casual fashion. The whole dramatic scenario held my fascination as we clambered back on board the helicopter. I held my eyes glued to the image of the magnificent structure shrinking as the chopper soared to the skies and watched it fade in the distance as we headed back to shore.

Travelling by helicopter, seeing the rig at first hand and appreciating the magnitude of the machinery involved all reinforced my feelings that I wanted to have a serious involvement in this oil business. The trip also confirmed my thoughts that I could not thrive in an offshore locale but would need to pick a path in an onshore environment more suited my preferences.

"Materials Supervisor" does not sound much of a prestigious position. At first hearing it brought to my cloistered mind an image of a nimble fingered spinster at one of our woollen mills shuffling hanks and bobbins, checking to ensure that the weavers would have the proper mix of merino and vicuna and whatever it was that went into making the cloth for the Crombie coats for which our city was rightly famous. It sounded incongruous when applied to a tall Texan such as Virgil Jeter, or the bustling Bill Byatt, but that was the title that described their jobs. In working closely with these guys as well as Stanley Adams of BP, John Snodgrass and Jim Allison at Shell and others over the period of 1971 to 1973 I arrived, eventually, at the view that this was the job that best suited my attitudes and aptitudes.

Following that trip to the *Sedco 135F* I would pester Bill and Virgil with a plethora of questions on how I could realise my growing ambition to join their circus and become a Materials Supervisor. Each responded as patiently and constructively as they could, giving me their sound advice and cautious encouragement but, as they were both aware of the gentlemen's agreement that they, as clients, shared with Jim Simpson, neither could make an outright offer of a position as a trainee or assistant that would help me to achieve my aims, though they did lead me to understand I would have to travel more, witness a wider range of drilling and exploration activities and learn a lot more about operations and equipment. I was beginning to form a clearer idea of where I wanted to go and what I wanted to be. I had not yet joined the Rat Race, but I was now tempted by the lure of the cheese in the mousetrap.

# 11. Onwards and upwards Part II

Ever since my first helicopter trip, whenever offered, I took as many opportunities as I could to travel and further my knowledge of oilfield equipment and experience of operations. I still had the wanderlust and longed to see the world and sample the events and delights that had been previously been offered only as vicarious pleasures. Without setting any restrictive kind of career path, I had set myself a target of becoming a Materials Supervisor within five years.

Within Asco, under the new ownership of Sidlaw Industries, the opportunities to travel were restricted to those places where the company had an existing involvement in shorebase activities or were seeking to develop bases along the east coast of Scotland. Sidlaw's key area of focus was very definitely on the construction and development of the South Bay Project at Peterhead with a lesser emphasis on our disparate interests in Aberdeen and Sidlaw's headquarters in Dundee. I could discount any interest in Peterhead or Dundee as neither place had ever held any attraction to my sensibilities. Although I did go along on visits to both places I never found anything in either that would whet my appetite for adventure and was becoming increasingly frustrated by the imposition of bureaucracy associated with Sidlaw's hierarchical structure..

Shetland presented a different scenario. I had been intrigued by the prospect of visiting the islands and, after my first visit, I was happy to return, growing more enthusiastic about working there. I would even consider settling somewhere on the archipelago. My first opportunity came when Imco (the new brand name for IMC) were asked by Shell and Amoco to supply their products from an island base. Imco had selected Lerwick as it was the biggest port and already being used by Shell. It seemed logical, following the successes of Lowestoft, Great Yarmouth and Aberdeen, that

Lerwick would be the "next big thing" and I was keen to get in on the ground floor. Imco had already positioned two mud silos on an outlying quay and had shipped in a consignment of barytes and other basic ingredients to an old warehouse in Lerwick.

Asco had agreed to despatch a bulker truck, a compressor, an auger and other accoutrements and had undertaken to support Imco's efforts in the Northern Isles. I had agreed to accompany Jock Smith on the northward journey on board the P&O ferry *St Clair* along with this kit and help to prepare the first load out of materials. There had been an advance party to oversee the initial stock-up of the warehouse but they had returned unimpressed by the islands and could not be persuaded to make a further visit.

In addition, as we heard at length from our recently appointed accountants, from Asco's new owners, Sidlaw, the initial visit had cost much more than expected and we would have to be more careful with expenses if they were to be encouraged to support future activities. As a consequence, Jock and I were booked on some sort of steerage deal that included discounted fares linked to the freight charges for shipping the plant. These discounted fares entitled us to our passage from Aberdeen to Lerwick, a bunk in a four-man cabin and nothing else. For the same price we could have flown to New York and back with free food and drink and money left over for a shopping spree.

As a notoriously poor sea-traveller I took the precaution of eating before embarking, staying on deck until out of sight of land and heading for the bunk as soon as the rocking and rolling overcame my ability to remain upright. Jock was a seasoned old sea-dog and felt entirely at home on the ocean wave. He showed his experience by laying first claim on the lower bunk, before heading for the galley where he stoked up on a high calorie supper of pie and chips.

By the time he returned from his supper we had been joined by another passenger, a tall, dark, fairly well spoken, reasonably well-dressed fellow with an accent that was difficult to place but clearly not Scottish. Jock spotted him as he opened the cabin door.

"Ay, Ay, min. Fine nicht, but the win's getting up an there'll be a bit o a swell. Peety ye're left wi a top bunk. Me an Johnny's tae'n the bottom anes."

"No matter, I will be quite comfortable wherever and I'm quite used to roughing it."

Our cabin companion may have been difficult to place but he was perfectly approachable and we chatted on about the weather, the waves, the cost of the ticket, the hardness of the beds, the heat from the adjacent laundry room, the creaky cabin door and the price of fish. Jock could also be quite sociable with a wide range of barely credible tales from his colourful background of contacts and exploits. With his immense bulk and blustering delivery he could appear threatening at times but over the years I had become inured to his ways. The stranger was neither here nor there and chatted away quite amiably. Jock reached into his suitcase.

"Here, Johnny, I've brocht ye a wee present fae the Bond."

Jock produced an unlabelled bottle of dark maroon liquid. I recognised immediately from the fluted pattern on the shoulder of the bottle and the black screwtop that this must be Watson's Rum and, as Jock had mentioned "The Bond," this must be one of the notorious "proof-samples" he would procure at moments of extreme duress. Watson's Rum is Aberdeen's own brand of rum and renowned among fishermen and sailors as the panacea for anything that ails a body. I had seen it, of course, served in pubs and parties, sometimes with blackcurrant cordial, ginger wine (Crabbie's preferably,) peppermint cordial or even Coca-Cola for the philistines. It was a strong, dark spirit with a heady aroma, a bittersweet taste and, given its high concentration of congeners, absolutely the worst contributor to a hangover headache, curable only with a hair of the dog.

How well I remember the occasion at the Coal Hole on a freezing January morning in the previous year. We were halfway through cutting a consignment of bentonite. For some obscure reason we had been instructed to mix salt with the light white powder of the bentonite clay. I know that common salt, sodium chloride, is hygroscopic, attracting water when exposed to the atmosphere. In a freezing atmosphere the water it attracts seems to turn to ice, especially if your fingers are in contact with the mixed powder, and the digits would become very painful before all sense of touch was lost completely. Wearing cotton gloves was no protection as the fabric would freeze and tear. In retrospect rubber gloves might have been the answer but we had none.

We had stopped at about ten for tea and rolls, which allowed a temporary thaw before we were dragged reluctantly back to our bulk cutting duties. What I then recall, with fond remembrance, after a further half hour of cutting and freezing, as the particles of clay and salt hovered in the air and settled on our clothing and on the equipment around us, giving the impression of a Dickensian Workhouse in Winter, was Jock Smith emerging through the misty gloom, with a sinister smile on his ruddy face, bearing a phial of a mysterious dark liquid.

"There ye are boys, that'll warrim ye up!"

"Fit's that, Jock?"

"Sshh! Dinnae let on! I got a sample oot afore the Customs manny got there!"

Ever resourceful, Jock had procured a sample from Watson's No. 4 Bonded Warehouse next door before the new batch of rum could be tested by the Excise man in preparation for bottling. In an act of human charity he brought it to his workmates, but first he had to certify its provenance. He took the small bottle, unscrewed the top and guided it to his cocked mouth. With only a minor twitch and a slight smarting of his eyes he pronounced the sample acceptable for popular consumption and passed the bottle on to me with a smile of endorsement.

I took the open bottle, dichted the top with my sleeve (hygiene and manners are important even in with a bottle of illicit hooch in a dingy warehouse) and took my mouthful. I recognised the taste straightaway but the stunning sensation was unprecedented. It was as if an electric shock was being transmitted through my body, however, this was no lightning flash, as the warming effect of the

154

elixir propagated in a wave-form working from my gut through my ribcage and outwards to my limbs. The whole experience probably lasted only a few seconds, but it seemed like minutes and before I could utter a word, my whole body was aglow and there was no sensation of cold in any extremity. My eyes were slightly out of focus but my body was restored and, somehow, we resumed the bulk cutting operation and had it completed by lunch.

"Giz roon yer hert like a hairy worm!"

Looking at the bottle now proffered in the cabin I appreciated that, in his resourcefulness, Jock considered a mouthful of "Proof" Rum, the world's best cure for frostbite, might also be a suitable remedy for seasickness and I accepted his invitation. Remembering my manners, I took the unopened bottle and gestured to our cabin mate whether he might also like a drop. He acknowledged the offer, smiled appreciatively, but declined graciously.

"No thanks, I'll pass. I should stick with my normal routine of a brisk walk around the upper deck, a read of a good book, and let the ship's motion rock me to sleep."

At that, he left the cabin and went on his tour of the ferry. While he was away Jock poured a couple of noggins, emphasising the benefits of rum in warding off nautical nausea. As I was already feeling queasy I lay flat out on the bunk and, recalling the powerful punch of the proof sample, took only a little amount. These sips had nothing like the restorative effect of my previous encounter; but that had been a rescue mission, this was more of a despatch and I was glad to feel slumber come upon me. Jock continued to test the sample and was getting quite garrulous. He liked company while drinking and was not going to let my tiredness spoil his fun.

"Here, Johnny, hae anither dram. This'll gie ye sea legs!"

"Just the one then, Jock, I'm needing my sleep. We've to be up at six, mind."

"Ah'll hae nae bother in getting up. Ah'll never get tae sleep in this heat. It's scumphishing in here. Mind you, the place'll cool doon fan thon mannie comes back. He's a right caul fish. Fit d'ye mak o im? Wi his posh spikkin voice, reading books—an' nae

155

drinkin? He's nae lik ony Shetlander I ken."

Our fellow passenger returned to the cabin, opening the door before I could venture any opinion. Jock was a little flustered at having his conversation interrupted and, with no other thought, offered each of us another drop of rum, which we both declined. Although not a drinking man our room-mate was no cold fish but surprisingly convivial and, as I maintained my prone position, he joined Jock at the small table and allowed him to carry on with his monologue. At times he would prompt Jock to elaborate on his stories and within a short time he had elicited all the information about who we were, where we had come from, where we were headed, what our business was and what we thought of Shetland's future role in the oil world. It was only at this point that Jock responded with any questions of his own although he had obviously been pondering on the fellow's interest.

"An fit de ye dae? Are ye in ile?"

"No, I am not in the oil business, but I am fascinated by how it might affect Shetland."

"Ye're nae a spy are ye? I hope ah hinna gied awa a wir secrets."

"No, I'm not a spy, and I have enjoyed the conversation but think I will turn in now."

"If ye're nae a spy, ye're nae in ile, ye're nae a Sheltie, cos ye're too posh spikken, ye're nae in the forces or ye widna be in the cheap quarters wi me an Johnny, fit are ye?"

"Oh, if you are going to be around Lerwick for a week or so, I am sure we will bump into each other at some juncture. You'll find out then. Good Night."

With that he then climbed to the top bunk, lit his reading lamp, slid the privacy curtain and settled down to his prescribed routine. Jock scratched his head, poured a large tot of rum and, as he always did whenever there was a gap in conversation, whistled and hummed a range of barely discernible sea shanties until he noticed that we had both switched out our lights. He ceased his serenade and rolled into his bunk.

I slept little that night, ill at ease with the ship's rocking and rolling and disturbed by Jock's thunderous snoring. It felt as if I had dosed only a few minutes when I was awoken by Jock giving me a shake to rouse me, but when I checked my watch, it was already six o'clock. He told me that as the ferry was approaching Bressay Sound I should get up and grab some breakfast before disembarking. As he had already washed and shaved, he hustled off to the galley. I stumbled slowly out of the bunk and noticed that our fellow traveller had also gone. After a quick wash and wipe I packed my stuff and wandered along to join Jock at breakfast. He was tucking into a sumptuous selection of fatty favourites, which ordinarily would have encouraged me to pile plenty on my plate, but the effects of the journey and the rum had not yet worn off so I restricted myself to a glass of grapefruit juice and a bit of toast.

We discussed our plans for the day ahead. Jock would take care of the truck and the kit and get it all to the warehouse. I would do some Customs paperwork before picking up a rental car and collecting the Imco man, Bob Allan, from Sumburgh Airport. I would also have to arrange for hotel accommodation for Bob and myself, but Jock said he preferred to lodge at the Seamen's Mission. This was near to the Thule Bar, one of his haunts from his previous visits as a fisherman, and he suggested this as a convenient meeting place for the end of our day.

My first sight of Lerwick, with its tightly confined cluster of ageing stone buildings, highlighted by the rising sun against a dramatic backdrop of stark heath, has left a lingering appreciation and in spite of my nausea and hunger it was with a sense of eager anticipation that I stepped ashore. Jock knew the town well and pointed out the Mission, Thule Bar and other landmarks. We went looking for accommodation and called in at a few hostelries only to be met with atypical inhospitality and told that nothing was available. We did receive an offer from the Grand Hotel at £26 per night. This was higher than my weekly wage so, as a point of principle, I declined. I did not despair but baulked at the prospect of sharing a night at the Mission with Jock.

We made our way along the North Road toward Bolt's Garage, where I picked up the cheapest available rental car, a yellow Mini 1275GT. Sometimes the cheapest option is the best and this was what transpired as I zipped along the south road towards Sumburgh. With no traffic, narrow carriageways, clear visibility and acute angles at the bends, driving in Shetland is a real pleasure and I revelled in the joy of guiding the jumped-up go-kart along the way without having to slow down for corners.

I collected Bob from the BEA flight. Following a scary landing, which I have since discovered is normal for Sumburgh, he appeared about as green as I had felt following my sea voyage and I was careful to drive back up the road in a more leisurely fashion. Bob had already made a booking at the new-built Lerwick Hotel at some exorbitant rate of £28 per night. That was one of the benefits of working for an international oil service company—they paid! As he was checking in I enquired, casually, whether they had any vacant rooms.

The hotel was always fully booked and hellish expensive, so I did not expect anything other than a cursory denial so I was glad to be informed by the ever courteous Assistant Manageress, Miss Goss, that, since this was Friday, the last flight had arrived and Shell had not confirmed their block booking, I could have a single room for £11 per night throughout the weekend, as long as I stayed no more than four nights. I nabbed it, knowing full well that I was booked on the return ferry on Tuesday night and the only alternative would be the Grand Hotel, which, from my initial survey was obviously a misnomer.

Bob was also new to the island and volunteered to accompany me on my calls to the Harbour Board and Customs House. We were both pleasantly surprised by our reception at both places. There was none of the pomposity or stiffness that I had witnessed with their counterparts in Aberdeen and everybody, exemplified by the jovial John Butler, the Customs Warehouse Officer, was welcoming and helpful. The paperwork was processed in no time and we looked forward to getting our work done without any anxiety or further fear.

We were strolling along Commercial Street when I spotted the familiar features of the tall, dark stranger who had shared our cabin on the *St Clair.*

"Hello there! You were right, you said we'd be sure to bump into each other."

"Why, hello again, Johnny. I am sorry I left without saying cheerio but your friend said you wanted a long lie. Did you have a good journey? Seen anything of Lerwick yet?"

I was in the process of expressing my delight at being in Shetland and my enjoyment at the early experiences when my attention was diverted by sight of an article of his clothing. His raincoat had opened as he took up a more relaxed pose revealing, behind his Fair Isle scarf, a mauve silk shirt and—a Dog Collar! A man of the cloth! It all fell into place and I had solved the mysteries that Jock and I had pondered over the previous night. The minister explained that he had been returning from a diocesan conference in Aberdeen. In order to protect the Church's stretched finances he chose to travel as cheaply as possible.We exchanged further pleasantries and strolled in our separate directions. I could not wait till I could let Jock know. It was approaching five and he would be waiting at the Thule as agreed.

"Hey, Jock. How's it goin? Did ye get a'thing intae the warehouse?"

"Aye, nae bother. Did ye find somewye tae bide?"

"Oh, aye, me an Bob's booked intae the Lerwick Hotel, wint tae jine us?"

"Nah, I'll be fine at the Mission. Did ye get a the paperwork sortit oot?"

"Oh aye, an I met wir mate fae last night on the High Street. Ye'll never guess fit he is."

"He's nae a bobbie, is he? Struck me as afa suspicious kin'!"

"Naw, Jock, he's a Meenister. Episcopalian."

"Fuck sake, I hope Ah wisnae sweerin, wis Ah?"

One of Jock's tasks that day had been to find a squad of labourers to help us with bulk cutting operations. We had heard it was a waste of time checking the Labour Exchange as even the locals would tell us that anyone on the "Broo" in Shetland would not be fit to do a day's work. The islanders have a proud and well-earned reputation for self-sufficiency and, in the range of chores necessary to maintain their boats, crofts, crafts and livestock, there is always plenty to do with no excuse for anyone to be idle. Jock reckoned he had a few old contacts from his fishing days and that we would be sure to bump into somebody at the Thule Bar. It was approaching five o'clock and a small burachie had gathered around the entrance in preparation for the start of the Shetland weekend, which is another fine tradition that deserves its place in folklore.

As the bar opened and we waited to get served, the buccaneering Jock made acquaintance with one or two who knew "so-and-so" and remembered working on "such-and-such" a boat trawling off Iceland or drifting for herring in The Minches, however, even after a couple of pints, he had not found anyone that could help us make up a crew of barytes cutters.

One of the patrons in the bar, overhearing our pleas, recognising our mainland accents and with a nearly empty beer-glass in hand, offered to help. We listened to his story, bought him another pint and started to discuss the job. From the derision of his fellow drinkers it was plain that they doubted his capabilities and, with the forthrightness and honesty that is typical in these parts, informed us that we had not only wasted the price of a pint but would also be wasting our time in hiring this particular native. His name was Billy Smith and he had just finished a seven-year stint in the British Army. This was verified by his mates but they also warned that he was a bit of a wild card, a fantasist and notoriously unreliable. There are no secrets in Shetland.

Billy then suggested that he could bring another helper along however, at the mention of this fellow's name (probably best that I have forgotten it,) the assembly was in uproar.

"Du'll nivver fit in wi dis ile crowd, Billy!"

160

"Diss is hivvy wark dese guys are wantin deen!"

"Du's pal's nivver din a day's wark in ees life!"

"An da pair o ye'll nivver get up on a Setterday, no efter a pairty!"

Billy lived up to his reputation as he shouted down the barracking horde, swearing that he would prove them wrong, the doubting bastards. We thought it better to leave at that point, drank up and bid farewell. Jock had secured his berth at the Seaman's Mission. Bob and I returned to the Lerwick Hotel but allowed Billy to share a taxi to his mother's house, which was on the way. Before he got out he reaffirmed his commitment to helping us out and arranged to bring along his buddy, fully kitted out and ready for work at the warehouse at eight in the morning.

True to his word, when Bob and I met up with Jock at the warehouse on the Saturday morning, there was Billy, decked out in Army fatigues, with a triumphant smile on his face and a faithful friend in tow. As I am a night creature and abominably slow to warm up until the day is halfway through, I hesitate to be over-critical of others in their morning appearance, but I did wonder how a person could look so unkempt, given that there were no hedges, as far as I knew at that time, in the whole of Shetland, through which he could possibly have been dragged.

This was a working party and not a formal occasion, so there was no need for pleasantries and we proceeded quickly to the job in hand. We had to fill each of the quayside tanks with fifty tons of barytes. With a few years of experience and a skilled crew, fifty tons was no more than a four-hour shift at our base in Aberdeen but, with raw recruits, we were prepared to take a little longer. As Bob was the customer, with a "Supervisor" at the end of his job title, we let him keep on his street clothes as he watched the action, counted the sacks and pressed the occasional button. Jock and I took turns on the fork-lift truck and helped out as required if Billy and his pal needed help with the sack-cutting. With a bit of coaxing and cajoling we managed to fill a bulker-load of ten tons by the first tea-break. Bob accompanied Jock to the harbour to see that the load was transferred successfully into the silo.

As Billy and I began to prepare the tea his buddy announced that he had had enough and could not carry on. Billy remonstrated with him and the conversation got so heated that, with my limited knowledge of the local dialect, I could not follow the exchanges. The upshot was that I had to part with a quid in payment of the fellow's labour and we were now a man short. Billy was embarrassed at being let down and applied his energy and pent-up venom to such an effect that we got on much better in the next session, completing two more loads before lunchtime.

I took advantage of the lunch break to go along with Jock to the quayside, ate my pork pie and downed a bottle of Dazzle as the bulker decanted the barytes into the silo. Sitting on a bollard, casually kicking the five-inch rubber hose that vented the compressed air from the loading operation, I admired the restful view. Along with the air escaping from the vent line there was a trace of dust that had seeped through the filters and I watched as it settled on the oil-stained surface of the harbour water.

I recognised a tall, bearded figure approaching from the pierhead. This was Jonathan Wills, a journalist from the Shetland Times. Like all self-promoting writers he was happy to have his visage presented on the page whenever one of his valuable articles achieved publication and that was at least twice a month. I liked reading the Shetland Times, as it was a quirky mix of aged news, prickly parochialism and surreal fantasy. Jonathan's pieces were usually well written with a left-wing slant on a range of subjects from pertinent political matters to esoteric meanderings on flora and fauna. He did not know me nor did I know him but, having read some of his musings, I anticipated his first question.

"Fit's dat du's pittin in oor wadder?"

"Oh, naethin tae worry aboot, harmless pooder."

He seemed dubious and I went on to explain the nature of the product as the same stuff that NHS patients with suspected ulcers might have to absorb before the X Ray that confirms or denies the evidence of a hole in their stomach lining. It was always a sound tack to invoke the NHS in defence of any argument with a Leftie, as no self-respecting Socialist would dare say a word against Nye Bevan's hallowed creation.

I would have welcomed some further discourse on the prospects and effects of oil development on his home turf but following my brief description of our operation Mr Wills seemed satisfied and proceeded to walk on toward the town without further questions. Not much of an investigative journalist, I thought as he walked on; I had had tougher questions from the jobsworth at the council landfill site in Aberdeen.

Our efforts in the afternoon session revealed a marked deterioration from our morning exertions and we struggled to finish the last two loads required to fill the silo. Billy was as eager as always to please but even his energy was beginning to sap and, as we despatched the bulker to the quayside with the final load, it was not with the expected sense of achievement but with a feeling of reluctance toward spending our Sunday in the same sort of slog. As we shut down the auger and sealed the hatch on the bulker we spied someone approaching through the open door of the warehouse. He was obviously a Shetlander, as he was wearing wellies and a boiler suit.

"Ay, ay, min, are ye needin something?"

"Na, I'm no needin' a thing, but I hear du's needin a hand."

This was our earliest example of the Shetland equivalent of the Bush Telegraph system and nobody, not even the native Billy Smith, knew who this was presenting himself before us, and we did not care to explore how he had discovered that we were, indeed, in need. He introduced himself as Magne Williamson, a building contractor from Scalloway, and he had learned that we might be looking for a team of workmen. He was a tall, well-built, hardy sort with a ruddy complexion and a ready smile who was obviously no stranger to hard work. This was good timing on his part and we were certainly in a receptive mood, although perhaps a bit sceptical whether there was any merit in introducing a third party at the halfway stage.

163

Magne asked all the right questions and seemed to understand what that was required. His assessment of the task in hand was impressive and he was confident that his squad could finish the job within a working day. Moreover, he had worked out that he could handle the outstanding fifty tons and would charge a flat fee of £50 for the job. Jock shrugged at the offer. Money was not his department. Bob was nonplussed. He had little idea of costings at that stage and was there just to ensure that we could deliver what the customer had ordered. I did a quick calculation and worked out that £50 was less than the cost of our board and longings for a day and thought it should be worth a try. We shook hands and agreed to start at 8am on Sunday.

As impressive as Magne's grasp of the workscope had been, his delivery on his promise was even more noteworthy. He and his crew had arrived before Jock and I turned up and needed little guidance in getting to grips with the machinery and the materials. The crew was a fairly stereotypical collection of islanders with their Viking appearance and a taciturnity that might have been interpreted as shyness, but in these circumstances was obviously an indication of their focus on their task. With only a few tips and hints from us, they had the pallets decanted, the bulker filled, emptied into the silo and returned to the warehouse in no time at all. They had the whole job finished before lunchtime. Jimmy Gallan and his hand-picked team had met their match. I was impressed but was forced to apologise as I explained that, as it was a Sunday and they had taken us by surprise and finished ahead of time, we did not have all the cash ready to pay them for their efforts.

"Dinna worry, du'll no get far awa wi'oot peyin yer wey on dis island."

Magne seemed content to wait until Monday. His squad would be working on building a new shed at Gremista and I could pick up the cash from the Clydesdale Bank and bring it out to him. This suited me perfectly, as I now had the rest of Sunday afternoon and most of Monday to relax and tour the island. I will not bore you with the details of my experiences of the sights and sounds. It was wonderful. Go and visit for yourself, you will not be disappointed.

I picked up the cash from the Clydesdale first thing Monday and sauntered along to Gremista and meet the squad as promised. They were in the throes of shed building with the steel frame and floor already in place.

Watching Magne's team in action at their speciality was awesome. They were builders but also manufactured their own building blocks, using a big blue machine that swallowed up sand, cement and granite chips and churned them in to a gooey mix. The machine spewed it into a metal grid before the men began furiously tamping the conglomerate into familiar block shapes. They then left the blocks to set and, once cured, would build the walls with them.

This was no Heath Robinson affair but a highly effective, economical, ecological device that I had not seen before nor have I seen since. I remember thinking if all builders would use such a device that houses and other buildings, like the sheds that Magne specialised in, would be produced in half the time, with much less fuss and at half the cost.

I could see now how they had coped so admirably with the barytes cutting and, on the few occasions that we required any more bulk handling, we would always call on Magne and his gang.

Although I had huge respect for Magne as an individual and his team's performance I recall an occasion on one of my subsequent visits when our friendship and business relationship was subjected to strain.

Following each other around, as the mud supply companies had always done, it was not surprising that Milchem would follow Imco's lead and decide to lay in stocks of basic supplies to Shetland. In order to obviate the punitive charges applied by P&O, who enjoyed a monopoly in traffic from the mainland to the isles, Milchem decided to ship a boatload of 400 tonnes of barytes from the mining facility in Foynes in Ireland directly to Lerwick. I was glad to be asked to join Ronnie Graver on a trip northward to supervise the offloading and delivery into a secure warehouse. There was a real shortage of warehouse space in Lerwick and, indeed the whole of Shetland, which helped explain why Magne and his squad were fully occupied and flat-out in producing building blocks to fill the gap.

Milchem had undertaken to find and pay for their warehouse while Asco were charged with the Ship's Agency along with responsibility for the material handling. I was fairly new to these demands but Ronnie had been through this in Yarmouth and Aberdeen so we remained upbeat. I had been lauding Magne's capabilities and assured Ronnie we would have no problems with any physical aspect, however, as all the pundits and harbingers of doom will reiterate, you should never assume anything.

There was a problem with the selection of the warehouse, which I must say was nothing of Ronnie's doing, as someone from his head office had fixed up the lease on a visit prior to our arrival. The appointed store was of granite walled construction with a cobbled stone floor that had been used previously for storing lamb fleeces prior to export from Shetland. Fleeces are light and compressible and can easily be stacked very high.

The store was tall and narrow and not designed for forklift operations. Sacks of barytes are compact and very heavy. When stored on wooden pallets they can be stacked at a maximum of about fifteen feet. Beyond that the weight of the material will crush the wooden pallets and there is a risk of dangerous collapse. I will not bother you with too many facts and figures about square footage, pallet capacities, turning circles and the like, but it transpired that the warehouse would not be big enough to accommodate all the incoming cargo and, with no alternative stores, we were left with no option but to stack the barytes sacks in a loose heap with no pallets.

This was manageable but was going to involve more human effort than we had considered. Turning to Magne, who would always be in attendance when required, I asked quite casually, as I knew he would have a ready answer, whether he could handle all of this for an equitable rate of, say £1 per Tonne.

"It'll hiv tae be an oorly rate. A tonnage rate winna wark."

"Fit wye nae, Magne, ye fairly scored the last time, fifty pound for four hours work."

Magne went on to explain, quite astutely, that in this instance the pace would be determined, not by his capable crew, but by the dockers and the harbour cranes and, as they both operated on an hourly rate, progress was expected to be glacial. I was forced to agree and, therefore, enquired what kind of hourly rate he would apply.

"Twa poond an oor is what we'll wark at."

"Two pounds an hour? Is that for a squad of three or four?"

"Twa poond an oor. Per man. Cash in hand!"

It took me a wee while to respond as I equated the hourly rate with other rates of pay in place at the time. Fifty pence was the rate that we had used in Aberdeen and could usually find enough people to do the job at that. £1 per hour was about what a tradesman would charge. We had seen a bit of price and wage inflation in the days since Decimalisation in 1971, and even our worthy GP's were threatening industrial action or professional inaction or whichever way you prefer to define withholding labour and had been holding out for a salary of £4000 per annum. I did a quick calculation and decided to play the NHS card.

"Two pound an hour? That's mair than a doctor's getting these days."

"Dinna see a lot a doctors hereabouts willin tae shift yer ba-right-ees!"

I tried not to explode and took some time to confer with Ronnie as to what we could do. We obviously had painted ourselves into a corner and were facing costs much higher than we had bargained for. Ronnie made a call to his head office, explained the situation and returned very quickly, announcing with a disconsolate shrug.

"Pay the money. There's nothing else we can do."

We paid the rate that Magne demanded. The job was completed and we all went home but I must admit that it all felt a bit flat and there was an element of sourness as I handed over the cash the next day. As events would turn out that would be my final trip to Shetland and that is regrettable as I would have liked to have continued to work there—and learned how to get along with characters like Magne Williamson.

The overwhelming problem was that there were relatively few demands for mud supplies out of Lerwick and I had to concede that Asco would have been wasting their time setting up there. This was a typical supply and demand scenario and something that militated against the future of supply bases in Shetland. It was too expensive to ship anything into the islands and too expensive to get simple tasks completed. Our customers had to apply a premium on to their list price for anything delivered from there. As a result the exploration companies preferred to pay the cost of supply boats sailing direct to the rigs from mainland bases.

Shetland also had bigger fish to fry and the lack of development in their supply bases was compensated by the much more suitable and successful development that became Sullom Voe.

# 12. Jobs for the Boys

As Britain froze in the dark in the wake of the first "Oil Shock" of 1973 the economy stalled due to higher input costs and closing factories. The boom that Aberdeen had been enjoying for about the past three years had spread to include the whole of the North East of Scotland from the Forth to Cromarty and even around to the forsaken West Coast. Wherever deepwater sites could be found to build the monster platforms required for producing our new oilfields there would be willing contractors to satisfy the needs of the hungry operators.

Professor Alex Kemp and his world-renowned team of economists at the University of Aberdeen have more than adequately furnished the statistics and defined the impact of the dramatic changes in the price of crude oil on the movement of people, incomes, house prices and air passenger movements, so I do not need explain all the details of what we earned, borrowed and spent. I can give you only my own account of how I responded to the vital economic forces and offer my view on how my family, friends and associates reacted to the most significant opportunity in Aberdeen's long and varied history.

For once in my life there was a real prospect of prosperity. With a fairly well paying job, a company car, a bit of travel and enticing offers of career advancement I had no more lingering doubts that this business was a winner. Though still not swallowing the hype that was being spewed out by the papers and television, I was reasonably convinced by the valid commentary from reliable sources and the evidence of my own eyes, as I toured the expanding onshore and offshore facilities, that North Sea Oil would transform our region.

Even after three years of solid improvements and forecasts of further fortunes, however, it was still difficult to convince those closest to me that this was a train worth catching. My elder brother, Jim, was a rare exception. He had jumped at the chance of going offshore and had plucked the fruits of higher wages, rapid promotion and international travel. Starting as a roustabout on the *Glomar III* he had risen through the ranks and was an Assistant Driller within two years, earning a salary in line with a doctor or lawyer. He was not the only one to reap the benefits and you would have thought that most of our generation would have followed suit but, as I recall, it was no easy task to overcome local prejudices. Possible contributory factors to Jim's willingness to sample the demanding itinerant lifestyle of a driller were that in 1971 he was unemployed, with a patchy work record and had a wife and three kids to support.

My younger brother Dougie held good educational qualifications, displayed a ferocious work ethic and, having served his apprenticeship as a Surveyor in the building trade, demonstrated a facility with equipment and materials. He would have been an ideal recruit for the offshore industry but dismissed any overtures that Jim or I made about changing his industry. Even though I remember him being disenchanted with his lot, while driving in his navy blue Ford Escort. singing along to Neil Young on his state-of-the-art Motorola eight track stereo;

*"Think I'll pack it in – buy a pick-up,*
*Take it down to LA*
*Find a place to call my own, that I can fix up*
*Start a brand new day"*

My family displayed all the classic signs of sibling rivalry and it was not unexpected that Dougie would automatically dismiss his older brothers' suggestions that he too, should join the offshore juggernaut. His temporary disenchantment with the building trade did cause him to leave his unappreciative employers at Hunter Construction. His career change was not, however, as dramatic as Neil Young's invocation and he joined fellow renegades Charlie

Mitchell, Neil Middleton and George Torpie to form MTM, which he has subsequently led to fame and fortune, not a little of which is down to the car parks and access roads that they have built for the office blocks and warehouses of the burgeoning onshore support of our oil business.

Friends are more amenable than family. That's why they are friends—right? Maybe persuasion is not one of my strong points, however, as I enjoyed no more success in convincing my closest friends to sample the joys and adventures than I had with my family. They say that the friends you make at school and university are the best and most loyal and, in my case, that has been borne out. The cousins George Cowie, Mike Cowie and Harry Barlow have been close chums since about 1962. Billy Grant, Ally Sangster, Bill Buchanan, Sandy Bowden, Stan Hepburn and Gordon Paterson have formed a tight circle of comrades from the time we shared the flat at 1 Devanha Terrace as students from about 1968 onwards.

With your best friends you can expect mocking and parody as part and parcel of the ties that bind and I have endured for decades "gentle" ribaldry about my inability to finish the course in Sociology that I had started in 1966 and failure to graduate as a Master of Arts. I was regarded as a dreamer, a dropout (with Honours.) Such badinage was exacerbated during 1970, as most of these guys completed their degrees and moved on in pursuit of further qualifications and professional stardom while I muddled along, filling in Customs forms and struggling with my attempts at learning to drive a fork-lift truck.

My best buddies were never going to be convinced by any of my comments that the incoming oil industry was to be any more attractive than any of the other transient opportunities such as hop-picking, prawn-peeling, wool-brogging, renting deck-chairs or fairground dodgems, all of which had been tried and tested and found wanting in terms of long term prosperity and job security. But there were no alternatives in austere Aberdeen in 1970. Mike, Ally and Bill opted to go on to further education and obtain the Diploma necessary to become school teachers. Billy, Sandy and Stan tried using their Honours Degrees to more meaningful ends, before also gravitating towards teaching. Gordon and Harry allowed their hearts to rule their heads and took off on their romantic quests to London and Cornwall. Only George Cowie was dragged into our new industry and, even then, belatedly and reluctantly, after trying to carve out a career in chartered accountancy with Williamson & Dunn.

Football was the focus of my sporting and social activities. My team-mates at Shamrock were all working class lads, mostly tradesmen of some sort. Henry "Oscar" Steele, Davie Wright and Jim Mills were time-served joiners, Dave Merson and Eddie Mannal were printers, Walter Baxter, George Leslie and Johnny Stables worked in the Meat Market, Dennis Foreman, Jim McPherson, Frankie Wilson and others worked in the mills. Only Ian Reid and Raymie Milne had office jobs.

As the only student and, later, the only representative of the "Oil" business, I would be quizzed about the wage rates, the conditions and the prospects in this new industry but any positive assertion would normally be met with disbelief or outright derision.

Youth, fitness and technical expertise were naturally all in evidence among my football friends, but I detected a noted reluctance to forsake "safe" jobs, home comforts and, most importantly, their weekly dose of football, to pursue alternative careers in what was generally regarded as a risky business.

The same applied with my new set of teammates at Hermes FC. Hermes was formed in 1968 by a bunch of football fans from the Rugby-playing Gordon's College, so they enjoyed the advantages of superior educational qualifications and, subsequently, better-paid occupations. Brothers Fred and Les Dalgarno, Dave Landsman and Sid Barrie were all solicitors, Les Hutton and Phil Benzie were teachers, Norman Law a stockbroker; Alex "Monkey" Forbes was an architect and his namesake Alex N. Forbes, who it was that introduced me to this fine group of lads, worked alongside me at Asco. Over the course of my three years with Asco, Alex and I introduced some of our contacts from the oil business into the

Hermes side but, in line with the experience with my team-mates at Shamrock, we never managed to persuade anyone to move out of the comfort zone of their traditional mode of employment and join the oilfield adventure.

While sharing a flat with my younger brother, Dougie, my University mates having abandoned Aberdeen for the big city attractions of London and Glasgow, I would move increasingly to mix in his circle of friends. They, too, were working class lads and, although football lovers, were not regular members of any team, preferring to spend the pre-match period in the pub and watch from the sidelines as they all roared and cajoled enthusiastically where, apparently, they learned more about the science and application of tactics and strategy of our national sport than those poor souls who spent their energies and efforts in pursuit of the pig's bladder. At least that is what it sounded like when we would convene in the Moorings or the Club Bar at five o'clock on Saturday afternoons for a pie, a pint and a post-match analysis.

On occasions our pub debates would progress beyond sex and drink and rock and roll to include discussions on our working lives and, once again, I detected a similar reluctance on the part of Dougie's gang to embrace the new wave of opportunity that was rolling in from the North Sea. The combination of expertise, wit and wisdom that I came across in this congregation of cronies merits a book, a play, a film and a TV series on its own but, for all their undoubted ambition and streetwise savvy, there was not one of them who picked up the pencil and ventured to make as much as a footnote in the screenplay presented before them.

Bob Nielsen was the senior member, aged about 30 and a welder who had become used to travelling far and wide in pursuit of better paying jobs or, in reality, any job at all. Bob baulked at the "hire 'em, fire 'em" philosophy of the oil industry. He had dabbled in some pipeline and construction yard projects but settled for the more predictable patterns of employment, albeit at lower rates, with the local blacksmith factories and shipyards.

His sidekick George "Dod" Snelling was fiercely ambitious and had also travelled the country seeking out opportunities but, as he recounted, would be taking a big chance by throwing in his new, salaried post as a Meat Inspector to start again as a roustabout. He had a wife and young family to support and a change of job was deemed too precarious. It did not stop him, however, asking me at just about every occasion we met whether there were "Ony Jobs?"

Dod's cousin, John "Zeke" Gray, was one of many joiners used to plying their trade on a seasonal basis and regularly decamping to London in pursuit of premium rates. Derek "Del" Shinnie and Ronnie "Bo" Milne were others who had also travelled to London but always grudgingly returned. It was Ronnie who came back with more fanciful tales than the others. His biggest claim to fame was that, by dint of his superior skills as a Shopfitter (rather than a mundane Shuttering Joiner), he had wangled a job at Shepperton Studios, where they shot the Doctor Who TV shows and had been responsible for building the Daleks.

Such wild imagination would have fitted right in with the pretences of the peripatetic prattlers who populate the platforms and rigs and amuse their fellow travellers with highly embellished tales of their experience and exploits. There is always a place in the oilfield for bullshitters. Ronnie has a brother, George, who had been one of the earliest to go offshore. George took his skills as an Instrument Technician and joined Schlumberger as far back as 1969. He developed his knowledge and skills before joining Leutert in 1974 as a workshop supervisor, working his way up to Managing Director and eventually owning the company, thereby making his fortune. Maybe it was Inverse Sibling Rivalry that inhibited the creative and ambitious Ronnie from following his brother.

Harry Mackenzie would have been in high demand with offshore recruiters given his valuable training as a Ship's Electrician. Bob Meres, Brian "Smudger" Smith, Kenny Hay, Les Bannister, Billy "Kookie" Reid and Davie McEwen all had apprenticeships and technical qualifications, the capability and the necessary drive to succeed but yet they all displayed hesitancy. They each had their own individual reasons for rejection as I recall.

"Ye canna get a pint efter yer work!" according to Harry.

"There's nae a bookie!" according to Kookie.

"There's nae Hairies!" bemoaned Bob and Les, who fancied themselves as "Ladies Men."

"I'd miss ma fitba on a Setterday!" was Celtic fan, Smudger's saddest refrain.

Davie McEwen was the closest to taking the bait and, ever since the first time he had expressed his bemusement as I turned up coated in barytes dust at a Shamrock training session, he regularly badgered me for details of developments, prospects and possibilities of this new business. His father Jimmy McEwen was the Janitor at St. Katherine's Club in West North Street where the team had its Thursday night practice under the watchful eyes of Bill Davidson, Bill Forsyth and Ian Leslie. Davie would join in enthusiastically with our four-a-side games and would occasionally play in the outdoor eleven but definitely showed a preference for the social side of the game. It was in the pub and parties afterwards that he would pick my brains and check out any opportunities.

Without doubt Davie had the attributes to make the jump and eventually he did, achieving fantastic success (which I will detail in a later chapter or maybe another book) but until 1974 he displayed the same caution and reserve as the rest of his many friends.

The trio of painters that comprised the "CMW" partnership was a classic case in point. The acronym derived from their surnames; Campbell (Brian), Morrice (Jim) and Wallace (Sandy) and their partnership was formed while they had all been members of Aberdeen Fire Brigade. Merely passing the brigade's entrance examination was testimony to their fitness and aptitude.

By setting up in their own businesses each had shown entrepreneurship and ambition, although only Jim had any formal training as a painter and decorator. Brian had started life as a GPO telegraph boy buzzing about on his BSA Bantam. Sandy had qualified as an engineer with one of the local mills. Brian did have a stint offshore in 1971 with IDC, where he rose quickly to the position of Derrickman, enjoying the challenge of the demanding working conditions and warming to the camaraderie but wary of the seasonality and insecurity inherent in this unpredictable venture. Jim was cautiously curious and quizzed me occasionally when we met, at parties or while CMW were engaged in decorating my new flat in Watson Street. Sandy, with his dour, dismissive nature put his rejection bluntly.

" Nae for me 'at ile game. 'At's nae real engineerin!"

Over a period of more than two years since I had first started extolling the rewards and benefits of obtaining an offshore job and placing a foot on the ladder of future prosperity, I can count on only a solitary success in my recruiting campaign, and that was with George Snelling's other cousin, Abbie Fraser. George, Bob Nielsen, John Gray and Abbie had all grown up as boys together in Kaimhill, where they went by the names of their Cowboy heroes, Bronco, Cisco, Zeke and Abe. You would have thought that their lifelong affinity with Westerns might have drawn them to the Texans in the oilfield but, in the shoot-out at the OK Corral, only the long, lean Abe went for his gun.

Sometime in late 1972, quite casually, in the normal exchange of our daily chit-chat, Virgil Jeter had asked me if I could find him some more warehousemen. Sedco were embarking on a new rig-building programme for the North Sea and would need to recruit some extra hands. They had already begun developing their first Training School, housed in the converted loft at Regent Road, under the expert direction of Professor Tommy Bicknell, who had been drafted in from the University of Texas. The school was aimed at fostering "Fast Track" recruits that would become the next crop of Drillers, Engineers and Toolpushers.

My first impression of Tommy Bicknell was quite favourable. In my role as Sedco's in-house freight forwarder I had the responsibility of arranging the importation to the UK from their Dallas HQ of the first BOP (Blow-Out Preventer) Simulator machine and had to arrange the delivery in time for his first course of instruction. He was genial and courteous, like most Texans, but with a more scholarly air, as might be expected from his title. I noticed, however, that physical handling was not in his job description as I arrived hotfoot from Airport Customs with his eagerly awaited piece of hi-tech kit and he left me alone to manoeuvre the 140-pound simulator into the appointed corner of the new classroom.

My huffing and puffing and under-breath cursing were met with Tommy's benign forgiveness and a gracious appreciation when I had finished. He asked me if I would be interested in joining his school, telling me they were looking for the same calibre of candidates in the UK as they would normally source in the States, by picking out strong, fit young guys with a bit of intelligence and a "can do" attitude who were prepared to travel the world along with the growing fleet of offshore units. I was flattered that he thought that I displayed such talents. One vital ingredient that Tommy mentioned and to which I had to admit a singular deficiency was the importance of a mechanical aptitude. The lucky fellows who comprised the first intake included Iain Mitchell, Brian Kessack and Charlie Cowe, none of whom were appreciably bigger or brighter than me but who could, each of them, get to grips with an engine, a winch or a pump with a certain aplomb. I have problems opening an envelope.

Virgil's quest for warehousemen was simpler. A facility with odd descriptions, long convoluted part numbers, literacy and patience are the essentials for a "Materials" man, "Parts" man or "Store" man as they were variously termed. I knew of only one candidate in my circle that appeared to fit the bill—Abbie Fraser. Abbie worked at Brake Services (Aberdeen) Ltd, picking and packing bits and bobs of automotive spares for the stream of clients who would come from a range of garages and repair shops around the town.

He was the most laid-back of individuals, never flustered even with even the most obstreperous truckers, mechanics or "gofers" turning up at his counter in the shop in Ann Street bearing a piece of mangled metal or fragment of shredded rubber and an anxious gaze, shouting *"Ahmneedingeenothemnoo!"* I had seen him in action, or, rather, in slow motion. Abbie did not operate at normal human speeds, though his razor-sharp wit indicated to everyone that he had sufficient intelligence to keep up in the most demanding of situations.

Virgil told me of his requirements on a Friday and had indicated that he wanted to make a quick appointment. I met Abbie in The Moorings the next day as usual, along with the rest of the regulars after the football. I explained what I knew about the job opportunity and asked him if he would be interested. Abbie asked the routine questions about rates and terms and I told him all I knew about the people and the prospects and, as he sounded convinced, I asked him if he could come to the office on Monday where I would arrange an interview.

To any Personnel Officer this would have seemed like a perfect match. We had an immediate vacancy, a willing employer and a perfectly well qualified candidate. The one thing that, patently, counted against Abbie's instant appointment as Sedco's latest ware-houseman was his abysmal attempt to appear trendy. Nowadays there is no need to follow fashion and a guy is allowed to dress almost as he feels. For some reason, peer pressure, personal preference or maybe just plain missing the point, Abbie had adopted the style of a hippie with shoulder length straight black hair and a bushy unkempt beard, wearing flared blue denim jeans, thick knit polo jumper and a herring-bone tweed maxi-coat. The end result was that he looked like Charles Manson might have done if he had woken up, hungover in a thrift shop and had to get dressed in order to make a hurried escape.

My own approach to personal presentation, I must admit, was no better and I did not stop to think about it before we turned up on Monday afternoon in the Sedco office, but I could detect from Virgil's expression and wry smile that not everything was quite as he had expected. As always Virgil was most polite and ushered Abbie to a seat, offering him a cup of coffee and informed me, kindly, that he would handle the interview on his own. I could return to my office where he would send Abbie when he had finished. I skulked away worrying that this perfect arrangement was not going to fall into place as we had hoped, equally concerned that I might end up disappointing both Abbie and Virgil.

My frantic fretting was misplaced, however as, after a seemingly interminable half-hour, Abbie appeared in my office with a broad smile. He and Virgil had got along famously and the job was offered and accepted on a handshake. There had been a little banter about the starting rate of only a reasonable £22 per week but Abbie was confident that he would see out the three-month trial period after which he could expect a significantly enhanced £26 (plus overtime.)

Virgil had handled the matter of Abbie's long hair and beard with gentlemanly tact, by explaining that, for safety reasons, all offshore personnel had to be clean-shaven and it was only fair to ask that onshore staff follow the same standards. By the end of the meeting Abbie had volunteered himself for a makeover and I barely recognised him when he turned up for his first day at Regent Road the following Monday, looking like a shorn sheep. The next time I met Virgil he gave me another of his sardonic smiles and shook his head wistfully.

"John Milne, you sure can pick 'em! He don't look like no oilfield hand but I reckon that our Hippy Storeman's gonna make it."

And "make it" Abbie certainly did, coping easily with his new duties as a shore-based warehouseman, before travelling to Port Arthur in Texas to join the construction of the *Sedco K*, later transferring to the *703* where he retrained as a Watchstander. Within a few years Abbie was promoted to Barge Engineer where his calmness under pressure proved to be a big advantage.

Abbie's adventures and improved lifestyle made some impression on the rest of our pals and, during 1973 and from then on, they began to think that there might just be something in this oil game. I started to hear some more positive responses from those who had previously dismissed it as a pipedream.

The rising general prosperity in Aberdeen meant that all

factors relating to incomes and outgoings rose in proportion to the increased activity and the wealth generated. Some long established icons, including buildings, businesses and ancient organisations were obliterated. A few hardened traditionalists can still be heard bemoaning their passing. Social scientists will now write their papers and opine that all this was the inevitable result of market forces and the disintegration of the extended family and parochial values. To the man in the street this was manna from heaven. Oilmen call it Paydirt.

We saw lorry drivers progress from virtual wage slaves to running their own fleets of trucks, carpet cleaners progressing to become facilities managers with a staff of hundreds, welders shedding their gloves and goggles and forming their own fabrication shops, receptionists casting off their nail-files and setting up their own employment agencies. I know plenty of examples but some of the people I am thinking of, who started off with so little then, are now so precious that I would probably need to seek them out for interview and clear their stories with their agents before I could put their name on paper.

I choose the word "precious" rather than "wealthy" quite purposely. Of all the people that I knew (and that is pretty much everybody who had worked in the very early stages of North Sea development) who did make the admirable attempt to plough their entrepreneurial furrow, there are none that I would say have made significant fortunes. Most achieved a standard of living that would have made their fathers envious and their mothers smile with pride. Some even attained levels of success that would have seemed unimaginable to their predecessors but, unfortunately, there were some who strayed or failed to stay the course, and we should not dwell on that.

There have been quite a few who have built impressive empires, some of whose stories are hagiographed in Jeremy Creswell's book entitled "Conversations with North Sea Moguls." Whereas I admire Jeremy's intensive research, his enviable work-rate and careful but

180

readable prose, I would baulk at his choice of the word "Mogul" in the book title.

That word, in my view, should be reserved for the marauding magnates in our industry, such as Rockefeller, D'Arcy, Getty, Gulbenkian, Hammer and Hunt and a few others, who amassed billions manipulating large sectors of the international oil market, before the emergence of the corporate giants who now control our fortunes. They were big fish in a big pond.

At time of writing our most successful local businessman is Sir Ian Wood and depending on the current state of the markets, all of which depend on the price of real assets, like oil, his value is rated at about £1billion or $1.4billion. Less than a year ago it was as much as £2.2billion and $3billion but such is life in this energetic enclave! I feel for the guy, I really do. He has a renowned intellect, a formidable work ethic, undoubted humility and a genuine concern for good causes, aligned with a record of success that is unparalleled in his home-town base, and probably hard to beat in the rest of the UK, or Europe to that matter.

Before you start imagining that I am some sort of acolyte or grovelling creep, clinging on to the patronage of the mighty Wood Group, or a former employee dependent on the resources of its Pension Fund, let me say that, although he is one of my local heroes I have never worked for him or even met the man.

If there is a point to all my rambling it is that until 1973 not many outside Aberdeen had heard of Ian Wood. The family was well known within the local community for its fine record in the fishing industry. The oil companies knew of the presence of the Wood family and their extensive resources within the much sought after harbour area, their access to quaysides and scarce warehouse space.

They enjoyed a valuable distributorship as Woodacon Oils with the mighty Conoco but they were seen to be standoffish to the overtures of the incoming explorers, from 1965 onwards, seeking to establish marine bases; that was part of the explanation why IMC, Baroid, Milchem and others beat a path to Jimmy Simpson's door.

Opportunities were there for entrepreneurs as well as employees and our local businessmen, with very few exceptions, displayed the same reluctance as their workers in adopting and adapting. It was not until some time in 1972 that Wood Offshore made a concerted effort to enter the shorebase service sector and, even then, with a modest investment of a small fleet of articulated vehicles under the guidance of Bill Lamb.

From their modest overture Wood Group have since composed a symphony of enterprises and enjoyed many encores.

With the continuing decline in traditional local industries and the inevitable loss of safe, secure jobs, the people in Aberdeen, my pals included, began to look toward the oil business as a better option. Throughout the periods of hyper-inflation in the seventies and eighties oilfield rates kept ahead of the national average. Terms and conditions improved to afford a safer and more comfortable working environment with more attractive work schedules and a raft of hidden extras. The side benefits of real worth included stock purchase plans and pensions, however it was peripheral benefits of corporate entertainment and frivolities such as Puffa Jackets, baseball caps and golf balls, emblazoned with company logos that attracted all the attention.

By the time of the second "Oil Shock." following the nation-alisation of Iranian assets and other events of 1979, several of my reluctant recruits had been drawn into the industry; I am pleased to report that most have survived and thrived. Bob Nielsen used his valuable welding codes with a variety of fabricators in some exotic locations. Harry Mackenzie applied his electrical expertise with various offshore maintenance contractors for more than twenty years and was canny enough to save enough money to buy a share in a pub. Les Bannister overcame his initial reluctance and has been employed in platform operations continuously for a period of over thirty years.

When I listen to these guys nowadays it seems impossible to imagine that they could have enjoyed comparable success in traditional occupations at home or, indeed, anywhere in the UK.

Only George Snelling took the emigration option, leaving for Australia in 1976. The joiners, Zeke, Bo and Del all stayed in their trade and managed to resist the call to go offshore or to drift back southwards, but happily concede that it was the steady demand for housing generated by the successive oil booms that allowed them to maintain employment in the city of their birth.

As I have not maintained particularly close contact with my former football chums at Shamrock I am not aware how many of those followed the Yellowbrick Road but I would imagine they followed a similar pattern. I did come across Henry Steele (Oscar) a few years ago at a corporate golf outing sponsored by Turner Diesel at the plush Letham Grange. We were both surprised but pleased to meet again and engaged in the usual exchange of enquiries among people of our background:

"Are ye still playin' fitba?" We were both by then in our fifties.

"Far are ye working?" We had not come across each other for over twenty-five years.

I was taken aback by Oscar's response. Not by the fact that he said he was now a Maintenance Manager with Elf (which explained why our hosts were fawning over him) for there are many other examples of local tradesmen scaling the heights in the offshore industry and I had considered him no less capable or confident than others. Oscar always has chutzpah to spare. Always. No, it was in explaining his creditable progress from offshore operative, gaining promotion to supervisor and being groomed for management that Oscar displayed a previously unheard of humility and asserted;

" I was lucky enough to get in at *the start* of this caper."

My surprise came in hearing that *the start* of Oscar's career was in 1975, which would be about five years after I would have first alerted him to "this caper" and about ten years later than the first real signs of oil exploration activity in Aberdeen.

The responses I received from Jim Morrice and Brian Campbell, when meeting up with them after a gap of a few years, are similar to Oscar's. They had moved on from running their own

183

decorating business to join the throng of offshore klondykers in the late seventies. Their previous training as firemen had given them a "leg-up" and, not unnaturally, they both progressed quickly through the ranks and are now very comfortably planted in their prestigious positions as Quality Assurance Managers or Health & Safety Executives or whatever titles their employers at BP and Talisman have dreamed up to justify paying them a hundred grand a year. Even Sandy Wallace swallowed his pride and joined the caravan and is currently an engineer with Shell.

Smudger, Bob Meres and Kookie also belatedly joined the trail into the oil business, all in a shorebased administrative context, and they seem to have thrived on the experience. When I see them today, after engaging in the traditional exchanges of football and sex and getting on to matters of work and money, it sounds like their entire working lives have been spent in this role. Such encounters set me thinking that very few people, even those of power and influence within this vast business, have acknowledged anything that had preceded their own introduction to the industry and these are some of the thoughts have led me to write down my own recollections of those early days.

Ignorance of the past can lead to a lack of vision for the future and this worries me. As we have passed peak production and are observing the decline in North sea activity we surely cannot simply say "that is it." We are presented with a range of opportunities to work on our experience and develop our skills in the new areas of oil and gas exploration however, in my view at least, we are facing them with the same lassitude and reluctance with which we greeted the arrival of the North Sea extravaganza. As Mark Twain said "History rarely repeats itself, but it usually rhymes."

# 13. Stag Nation

With all the wonderful success stories of local worthies, myself included, achieving wealth and fame beyond the dreams of their kith and kin, it may seem petty or churlish to bemoan the fact that we all took more time than necessary in getting our act together; nevertheless, I would like to emphasise my point that people from Aberdeen and the North East are dangerously slow to notice and react to changing circumstances, none more so than the local authorities, but also the band of businessmen by whom we all have laid great store and who, significantly, failed to cash in on the biggest opportunity of their entrepreneurial lives.

The popular view is that Aberdeen and its hinterland enjoyed so much success because it proved particularly receptive to the incoming oil business. My observations lead me to a different view and I hope I have helped to illustrate this in some way with the preceding tales of a few of my contemporaries. In hindsight I wish I had given more attention to my own involvement so that I could have better persuaded more of my family, friends and associates to shake off the shackles, forsake home comforts and join this circus of fun, fame and fortune but console myself that, at least, I and a few others have given it a go and have enjoyed the ride.

As I have consistently failed over my long working life to get to grips with political infighting or learned how to succeed in any bureaucratic organisation, it is of particular regret that I could never get myself into a position to exert influence on any of the law makers and decision takers who mould our working and social life. Maybe I could have imparted the knowledge and wisdom gained from those informed incomers who were aware of the offshore bonanza and happy to share the spoils with their onshore supporters and persuaded the powers to offer a more positive response.

The penny dropped eventually with most of my sceptical pals, and many have levitated themselves from tenement torpor to suburban splendour, but I am still unsure as to whether the officials in the local authorities have ever grasped the significance of the impact of the oil business to Aberdeen's past and, more importantly, its relevance to our continuing prosperity.

Okay, councils, chambers and committees are often dismissed as dithering dinosaurs and it would be too easy to pick on them but surely our highly regarded and, by 1973, with banks scattering cash in every direction, well funded entrepreneurs should have been heading for the high board and making a big splash in the pool of opportunity?

Again, not in my experience, I'm afraid to say; and that is not a complete damnation of the spirit of adventure in Aberdeen and the North East. Over several centuries we have produced many fantastically successful and well-recognised pioneers and adventurers of which our region can be justly proud; people like Thomas Glover and Bertie Forbes have risen from humble beginnings to create businesses that have driven and dominated world markets. It just seems that although our home-grown entrepreneurs have attained enormous success and high acclaim in overseas arenas they have consistently come up short in their own backyard.

In the period from 1965 to 2005 the most significant and successful individuals making a notch on the North Sea scoreboard have come from outside the area and with the notable exception of Sir Ian Wood there are none who have used the springboard of success in the North Sea to go on and make any kind of impression on the world stage.

I am not much of an entrepreneur myself but I have dabbled and, I think, given a fair account of myself (won one, drawn one, lost one.) As far back as I can remember I have shared with many the patriotic admiration in following the fortunes of our fellow Scots who have climbed their individual ladders of success. Most of my early inspiration came from reading "The Honest Truth" columns in the Sunday Post written about self-made millionaires starting with nothing but a basket of buns and ending up with huge factories producing Tunnocks Teacakes or Lees Macaroon Bars. You can see where my tastes lie.

Should you require a more erudite dissertation you might care to read the works of Niall Ferguson, Tom Devine and David Stenhouse on the exceptional determination and domination exercised by our industrious progenitors in carving out The Scottish Empire (otherwise described as the British Empire or World Commerce.) These books take a bit of reading but if you have the time and perseverance you should come to the same conclusion as they did that we, as a nation, are good at exploration and exploitation and it is surprising, therefore, to note that, when presented with an opportunity on the scale of the Union Pacific Railroad or in building the Japanese Navy which, in equivalence, has been the North Sea Adventure over the past forty years, we have not fostered another Forbes, grown another Glover or created another Carnegie.

As most of my peer group comprised working-class lads who grew up in a fairly depressing Post War environment it is perhaps forgivable that they should settle for steady, secure jobs. Within my circle there were only a few who displayed an enterprising streak and preferred to be self-employed. Some regarded them as "chancers" and in a previous generation they might have been termed as "spivs," but every society, capitalist or communist, needs such people of imagination to oil the wheels and fill essential gaps in markets.

There were two in particular whom I met while playing at Shamrock who, although completely contrasting in most aspects, shared the common goal of self-sufficiency and the drive to succeed on their own efforts rather than on the coat-tails of others.

Tom Riach was tall, fair, urbane and invariably neatly dressed, favouring pin-striped suits, cotton shirts and silk ties. He was two years older than me and had been an old classmate of my brother, Jim, who it was that had first alerted me to Tom's redoubtable prowess as a footballer. In stretching to his six foot three inch frame, Tom had sacrificed some of his adept ball skills but none of his physical competitiveness. I recall a match that Shamrock played against Inverness Thistle, earning a creditable 3-3 draw during which Tom negated the mighty presence of the legendary Willie Grant and received much deserved kudos.

It was Tom who had been my driving instructor and guided me to passing my driving test and for this alone much thanks. During our conversations in the course of those lessons I gleaned a glimpse of his entrepreneurial ambitions.

Tom had achieved some experience and reasonable rewards in selling office equipment, had had a stab at running an employment agency and was keen to try something innovative that would generate income as well as intellectual stimulus; he would quiz me about my contacts in this new oil caper. Although I was paying £2 per hour for the privilege, while trying to maintain my focus on the "mirror, signal, manoeuvre," mantra and attempting to perfect my three point turns, I took on board his other interests and made a mental note to help out if I could.

Ian Maitland was the antithesis of Tom Riach. Short, swarthy, with a quick wit and a temper to match, Ian was one of the George Street Mafia with strong connections to the Dee Swimming Club, via Richards' Mill (different story, another book, possibly) thereby to Bill Davidson, our Trainer. He would join in the Thursday training sessions at St. Katherine's but, as he was a bit older, he was disqualified from playing on a Saturday. He was a notoriously hard worker, running a small company that performed all sorts of jobs, cleaning houses and offices but mostly shampooing carpets. Ian was kind enough to respond to my request to help find a casual job for my student flatmate Ally Sangster in a time of need. Anyone who knows Ally will testify that he is one of the most diligent, energetic and uncomplaining of folks; however, at the end of his carpet cleaning stint in April 1970 he avowed to me, part in thanks, but mostly in disbelief;

"See that Ian Maitland, he's nae real! Nae mair shag pile an' shampoo for me!"

Ally and Ian certainly represented a match for each other and both appreciated the mutuality of effort and reward as I have since learned. I too remember favours and always endeavour to repay where I can and so it was that, in late 1972, during my regular stint as Customs Clerk at the Shell office, when I heard of a business opportunity, my thoughts turned to those who had earned the right to gain the benefit of my inside knowledge.

One of the most joyous of benefits of working, even as a Contractor, in the Shell office was the regular provision of free coffee—and biscuits. Everybody else, including Councillors and Civil Servants, had to pay for their office refreshments and often had to take part in preparing and serving (which may be the source of the clichéd response of how such people end up in the hallowed institutions sponsored by taxpayers.) In the Shell office, the coffee was freshly made, poured and presented on the dot, at two minute intervals after the appointed hour of 10am in a china cup (Wedgwood or Denby, depending on level of seniority) with a teaspoon to hand and a ready smile, from the ever obliging Mrs Walker.

I held a special regard for the marvellous Mrs. Walker, not just for her pleasant demeanour or out of deference to her age and gender, which was *de rigeur* in the seventies but strangely inadmissible nowadays. My appreciation relates particularly to the extra effort she made in reserving my favourite Bourbon biscuit with my morning coffee. Now that is a signal lesson in customer service! But Mrs Walker was due to retire and, in the spirit of progress, Shell had decided that, with plans to expand, this key position should be contracted out.

Albert Abela performed all the offshore catering and victualling services on the *Staflo* rig and had first option but, unusually, could not find a solution. The office services company who did the cleaning could not find a suitable candidate and somehow the question arrived at my desk. Did I know anyone?

I took the idea back to Regent Road and asked everyone there but, as things were heating up generally all around the town, this

189

was deemed a task not worthy of serious attention. Asco were looking at bigger kettles to boil.

My thoughts turned to offering an opportunity to those who had been badgering me for an entry into this expanding oil sector. Tom Riach had a little involvement in office services and got the first call. He thanked me graciously for the invitation, but, with appropriate wit, said it was not quite his cup of tea.

Not so with Ian Maitland. As soon as I suggested it he snatched at the offer and made an appointment within the hour to meet with Stan Brands, whose responsibility it was to ensure that the Shell office was fully staffed and catered for.

Of course Ian did a great job of meeting the demands of his first "Oil" client and enjoyed the benefits of greatly increased business as Shell expanded into their new offices in Altens. He now had hundreds of thirsty customers and revelled in the prospect of further expansion. Within a year he had also secured other office service agreements and Standard Cleaning Contractors were well on their way to stardom. By the end of the decade, Ian had added a general supply outfit, SCC Rig Supplies, to his portfolio, and was driving about in a white Rolls Royce Silver Spirit (500 PG.) Hard work and customer attention were all that was required.

Jim Simpson remained as my role model in the entrepreneur stakes. Although he did not display the same work ethic as Ian Maitland (he had Jimmy Gallan to do all of that) he was the first person that I had met who understood completely the need for exceptional customer service and, with very limited resources, that is what he delivered. By 1972 Asco had a client base that was the envy of all in the oil service sector; however, in spite of wholehearted efforts by all involved, we were losing out on the contracts we had striven to secure over the past five years.

Outside competition in the form of Offshore Marine, Hudson Freight and Nimmo had moved in to take sizeable bites out of the pie that we had prepared and cooked and should have had to ourselves. Local companies with deeper pockets, Wood and Ariel, were muscling in on the act, and new entrants like Seaforth Maritime and Norscot appeared on the scene. Some of our major clients had despaired of Asco's ability to deliver on their early promise and had gone on to develop their own facilities; Amoco to Pocra Quay, Conoco to Dundee and Sedco to Tullos.

As we were a small family unit we were all quite aware of Jim Simpson's shortage of monetary backing and shared his embarrassment at the lack of support we received from the local authorities and it was no surprise, therefore, when we heard he was seeking new partners. It came as a bit of a disappointment, however, when we found out that the favoured backer that Jim had selected to springboard our dive into the big pool was not one of the blue chip contractors nor any of the high flying Merchant Bankers that had been courting Asco during the heady hype pervading the Oil Boom but Sidlaw Industries, the old established Dundee firm with fading fortunes in the Jute Industry and a tenuous link in packaging. None of us had anything like enough experience or knowledge of business matters to make an informed judgment, but something did not ring true when we met our new venture partners to find that they all spoke in plummy accents, wore suits and regimental ties, called each "Mister," or "Sir," and arrived for Board Meetings in chauffeur-driven Daimlers.

Over the course of events, Jim did explain the necessity of sound financial backing, working capital, cash flow and operating systems, whatever they were, and as a committed team, we all tried to fall in line. With the benefit of hindsight, and having since acquired a working knowledge of business finance, I can see that the involvement of Sidlaw was something of a rescue mission and that Asco might have simply disappeared under the waves if we had not jumped on to their ark; nevertheless, in my naivety, I found myself becoming very uncomfortable with their attitudes, philosophies and revised ways of working.

Sidlaw made all the right noises about helping us to maximise the fantastic opportunities that Jim Simpson had unearthed, and the wonderful reputation that Jimmy Gallan and his crew had earned, but, in practicality, they were just a stodgy old Scottish industrial dinosaur with outdated principles and stultified practices. A business consultant from Urwick Orr & Partners, the leading experts in modern efficient office systems, was brought in to analyse and streamline our organisation. I forget the chap's name, but remember sitting with him for about an hour and a half in our lean-to office at Regent Road, as he detailed all the duties, tasks and responsibilities involved in my daily routine and made occasional notes in fountain pen on a foolscap pad. I had expected a slide rule or a calculator at the very least.

Our business efficiency expert spent equal time, making similar notes, with Alex, Merv, Graeme, and Ed Robertson. Ed was a bit older than the rest of us and had recently returned to his native Aberdeen following a spell in Canada, where he had been Inspection Supervisor at a refinery. With his considerable nous and oil experience you would have thought that he would have found a better-paid job than helping out with the dockside duties that filled our working day, but Ed was a realist and recognised that better positions were not yet available in Aberdeen.

He was also sufficiently clued up to know that there would be positions aplenty before too long. From his experience in Canada, Ed held a cynical view of business consultants and their analyses and he forecast that the outcome would be a more rigid, hierarchical structure with Sidlaw managers in key positions and Asco minions reporting to them, and that, I am afraid to say, is just about how things panned out. Ed left soon afterwards to pursue his career elsewhere. The rest of us continued to apply our limited knowledge with the same enthusiasm, our ambitions fuelled by promises of bigger and better things to come.

In fairness to our new leaders, in spite of all their turgid business meetings, boring budget reviews and their laughable attempts to integrate Jim Simpson's magical elixir of anarchical enterprise with the cold porridge of their hierarchical bureaucracy, they did manage to deliver the plum prize of the South Bay Development at Peterhead. It is only in retrospect that I can fully appreciate the magnitude and consequence of this achievement, as South Bay represented in 1972, and remains today, the best designed and equipped supply base for the support of offshore exploration and production activities.

We might have mocked as the patrician Sidlaw board members, with more letters in their titles, forenames, qualifications and honours than their entire surname, arrived from Dundee in their limousines, driven by forelock tugging lackeys, and would have dismissed as risible the possibility that they could engage with the plain talking, pragmatic pioneers that we had come to know at the sharp end of the drilling industry, but we had to acknowledge their connections in high places within UK authorities.

As we discovered, with wariness on both sides, all negotiations with the major clients were left in the capable hands of Jim Simpson and Jock Munro. It would be a different scenario, however, when it came to planning and designing our facilities on our prized asset at South Bay. Even allowing for the government grants that came with the planning permission, this was to be a mighty £2-£3 million investment, and our careful new owners were not about to let go of the reins on that scale of expenditure. Under the watchful eye of their implanted Chief Accountant, Alex Fraser, we were taken to task on every single expense and his austere approach to financial reporting came as a culture shock to us all.

Withstanding the forces of bureaucracy and railing against the infuriating interferences of petty-minded legislators and accountants are part and parcel of how Scots have come to dominate world commerce and my own tendency has always been to attack such obstacles to enterprise with quixotic zeal. Tilting at windmills is an acknowledged weakness, and I have to admit a signal failure in my attempts to persuade our new owners that there was merit in a more relaxed approach. My frustrations in trying to cope with the imposed strictures contributed to my growing disenchantment with my working life. I had joined this circus with a view to moving on, having some fun, seeing the world, enjoying adventures beyond the scope of my restrictive local environment and, although I was delighted that the oil world was now beating a path to our door, I had hoped that this would bring a change of attitude and improved working conditions.

Disappointingly, the Sidlaw approach proved to be as dull and uninspiring as the first impression conveyed. Weekly management meetings were introduced and all the office staff would decamp to the Dee Motel for a business discussion over a sumptuous lunch. As much as I have always loved my food and have grown to love business, this early introduction to "Lunch and Learn" was too much to take on board and I could not wait to get out of that stifling atmosphere, where everybody paid attention only to themselves and to their perceived superiors.

Evening meetings proved to be worse, as the same rules applied, with everybody blowing their own trumpets and attempting to crawl up their boss's arse without any consideration of clients' demands nor any appreciation of the workforce's efforts. The only difference was that there was no dinner on these occasions and that made them doubly hard to endure.

There were some encouraging aspects to the Sidlaw takeover however. One was that we now enjoyed the attention of the local authorities. I remember taking our Chairman, "Geordie" Cox (the one with the four initials before his name and many more behind it,) along with Jim Simpson on a visit to St Nicholas' House for a meeting with the Planning Director. It was only about 400 yards from Regent Road and a pleasant walk for anyone, but our Chairman insisted that I should take them in the Jaguar and pick them up when they emerged an hour later.

The big difference I noted was not just the fact that a senior council official would entertain a visit from Asco, when Jim had been pleading in vain for five years, nor was it the ability to cock a snook at the traffic wardens as I waited in Broad Street. "Waiting for the Chairman," worked a sight better than "I'll only be five minutes while the wife's at Markies."

No, it was when they emerged with beaming smiles and announced that we could now proceed with our adventurous building plans for South Middleton Base in East Tullos, that I realised that these boring old farts with bristling moustaches and hoity-toity accents might have something to offer after all.

The plans proposed and accepted for South Middleton were but a watered down version of Jim Simpson's original "Happy Valley" concept, but they were a welcome step in the right direction. As I had been working quite closely with Virgil Jeter, Bill Byatt and Ron Ball on the *Sedco 135F*/Amoco/Conoco exploration project, I think I had picked up on what these clients needed to satisfy their ambitious and demanding programmes and we all shared Jim's despair at his ability to convey those ideas successfully to, or elicit any positive response from, our local authorities. Now, mysteriously, dreams were becoming reality. The machinations that resulted in the approval for the Peterhead South Bay Project were in a different league altogether and only after many years did I start to comprehend how it was achieved.

By the end of 1972 Jim Simpson had sold his company to Sidlaw, had been awarded the MBE for his stalwart efforts in promoting the North Sea phenomenon and had his story told in "The Honest Truth" in the *Sunday Post*. His real friends were all delighted with his eventual successes although the amount paid by Sidlaw was a meagre pittance when compared to our view of his genius and pitifully inadequate when compared to other valuations of contemporary enterprises. His MBE was appropriate (colloquial translation – My Bloody Efforts) but was received with muffled congratulations by his envious peers in the Aberdeen establishment.

In his one-page life story in "The Honest Truth," Jim expressed his humble appreciation of the support of his family and his loyal workers and admitted that he was in awe of political processes, appreciating that his success had allowed him to obtain a glimpse of the corridors of power "but not yet the carpeted bits."

Our success in Peterhead allowed us to open our imagination and begin to consider serious expansion including further bases. There was a real demand for quayside facilities and storage yards and the hunt was on for new facilities. The premium non-tidal sites on Tayside had been commandeered by The Dundee Perth & London Shipping Company (DPL) and allotted to BP and Conoco. Peninsular & Orient (P&O) had secured the lesser-equipped, but conveniently sited premises at Ferryden in Montrose. My own hometown, in spite of the inattention of Aberdeen Harbour Board and the other complacent authorities, was overcrowded already, and operators without their own quay space had to queue and pay premium rates to ensure that their costly offshore operations could be supported.

All the east coast sites with navigable harbours, Fraserburgh, Invergordon, Wick and Scrabster were being considered and there was even talk of reviving old fishing ports like Stonehaven, Collieston, Burghead and Hopeman. Crazy thinking. Lerwick and Kirkwall were given more serious consideration as they lay closer to the more northerly oil discoveries and I was delighted when asked to go on a scouting mission as Asco's representative to determine whether we should add Shetland to our expanding portfolio of bases.

This was a boost to my self-esteem. Not only was I being allowed to travel by British Airways, rather than hitching a ride on a charter flight, or pitching and tossing on the P&O ferry, I was also allowed to book a rental car and make a hotel reservation rather than scratching around looking for vacancies in B&B joints. Asco gave me a £50 advance on travel expenses. With my three-piece Hepworth suit, Rael Brook shirt and Viyella tie I imagined I was quite the young executive and that I had taken a step up from my previous trips to this northern isle.

Shetland held a certain allure to my curious tastes. The stark treeless landscape bordered by precipitous cliffs and spectacular voes seized my imagination. The driving winds and soaring seas crashing on to the shingle beaches added to the drama. I had a fascination for the people, admiring their distinctive fiddle-based music, laconic sense of humour, delivered in their delicious lilting tongue, as well as their practical approach to problem solving and indefatigable commitment to self-sufficiency. There was a very small population of only 17,000 scattered throughout a cluster of islands and some considered them diffident and parochial. I have always found Shetlanders to be very open and welcoming and better informed in world affairs than most people on the mainland. I was looking forward to the visit.

As the Vickers Viscount descended alarmingly, weaving and lurching through the swirling gusts on its path over the surf and through the stacks on to the small ribbon of land known as Sumburgh Airport I gazed on the familiar brown scrubland dotted by feral sheep and picked out the slender silver strand marking the single track carriageway northward to Lerwick. I knew I had one of Bolt's Garage's rental cars waiting and hoped it would be their Mini 1275GT so that I could enjoy a belt along the twenty mile stretch of clear road, taking the tight curves flat-out with no fear of collision. As there was rarely any oncoming traffic, you could see for miles ahead; Shetland was great driving terrain.

There was a slight problem when I went to pick up the rental car. Bolt's previous customer had been over confident with his emulation of Paddy Hopkirk and had run it into one of the drystane bridges that cross the burns along the way. I would have to settle for a Morris Marina, British Leyland's cheap imitation of the Ford Cortina. No matter, it would be interesting to try out a new vehicle and I would have something to respond with in the bar room chatter with other reps when they asked the inevitable opener "What are you driving these days?"

There was a further problem as it had started to snow. My concern was that the Marina was rear-wheel drive and would not handle as predictably as a Mini, say, on a snow-covered surface. The Bolt man told me not to worry as, with the prevailing wind and the high salt content in the air, no snow would lie for long.

He was wrong—and right. By the time I had driven ten miles, as I approached Sandwick, there was total whiteout with no visible road markings other than the poles marking the drainage ditches at either side. I tried to slow down enough so that I could focus on the steerable path but, as I dabbed the brake pedal, the rear wheels locked and I lost control, drifting into the left hand ditch. After trying a few prescribed procedures, to no avail, I started to worry about being stranded and freezing to death in this remote island.

There was little time, however, to develop any overwhelming thoughts of doom and despair as I moped in my Marina and spotted, through the flurried mist, the familiar red blob of a Post Office van, pootering along on its rounds. The Postie noticed my plight and pulled alongside. One thing I like about Shetlanders is their directness, their ability and willingness to get to the point without any small talk or obligatory questions.

"Du's just cam frae Sumburgh. It's a winder du's got dis far—in a Bolt's car!"

Without further ado, but smiling all the way, he handed me a shovel, showed me where to dig, stuffed some sacking under the rear wheel and guided me on my way as I got in the car and steered out of the ditch back on the road. He sent me on my way and assured me that I should have no more problems since the snow would be gone before lunchtime and indeed, as I wandered wearily into the car park at the Lerwick Hotel, it was already starting to clear. By the time I had checked in and sat down to my egg mayonnaise the landscape had reverted to its familiar brown hue.

As much as I appreciated Shetland for its many attractions and benefits, I had to conclude that, regretfully, there was no sense in Asco expanding into the islands. By 1973 it was already overcrowded and all the best development sites had been nabbed by others. Inchcape were established at Gremista, Shell had major plans for Sullom Voe. Scalloway was out of the question and Hudsons were wasting their time thinking about Sandwick Bay.

On my flight back to Dyce, I began to realise that things had changed. In contrast to Shetland, Aberdeen was the Big City. But the Oil World was much, much bigger than either; it had arrived on our doorsteps simultaneously and had transformed both beyond redemption. The early diffidence of our northern cousins had transformed into fierce resistance and Aberdeen's local worthies had fallen into puppy-cuddling compliance.

All of a sudden Councillors were laying out red carpets, planners were releasing swathes of land, politicians were lauding the new spirit of enterprise, pubs were offering ice with the drinks and the cowboy culture allowed those who thought that this was Dodge City rather than the Granite City to stroll down Union Street in buckskin jackets, plaid shirts, Levi Jeans and high-heeled boots greeting each other with a "Howdy?" rather than the customary "Fit Like?"

My return to the Asco office was not like a dove to the ark nor as a lunar astronaut to a salutary splashdown in a Pacific paradise; it was more of a "where have you been?" type of experience, as everyone was steadily focussed on the pig trough that had opened in Peterhead. In my view South Bay was the ultimate in its potential as an offshore supply base and undoubtedly the most fantastic opportunity that the fledgling Asco could ever have contemplated, but there was something in the whole scheme of things that left me completely cold.

It was not just the hassle of negotiating the payment of my expenses on my return from Shetland. Alex Fraser insisted on the production of receipts for every incidental expense, not realising that the restaurants, bars, shops and taxis in Shetland had not yet been alerted to the paper culture that dominated the rest of the UK and would scoff at any request for a receipt.

It was more that, when I tried to feed the ideas that I had gleaned from my exchanges with our clients and the other intelligent, interested observers in this blossoming business, I realised I was misplaced in the Sidlaw regime.

At one of our management meetings, when the discussion turned to the allotment of roles in our revised organisation, I baulked at the predictable prognosis and made the suggestion that, instead of following the traditional path of waiting for business to come in the form of customers' orders and dutifully obliging by following up with suppliers' invoices, we should be offering a form of total material handling package, taking control of all the

199

customer's purchasing and logistics and charging on *ad valorem* or tonnage basis.

My suggestion was met with blank stares from the unaware and with outright derision by those who were then in the position to take this idea and develop it in harness with our very rich and very eager clients. It would have been nice even to receive a patronising nod but that, alas, did not transpire. It would be twenty years before I could award myself any gratification and that came when Colin Manderson, the incumbent Managing Director, promoted just such a strategy when he introduced the revolutionary "Integrated Logistics System," to great acclaim from his customers and shareholders alike.

Our new owners had tried to involve the junior officers in the process by sending Alex, Graeme, Merv and myself to planning meetings on the development of South Bay. The project was led by the cheerless, chain-smoking Charlie McGregor, an ex-BP manager with an impressive track record of major works in the Middle East. His achievements speak for themselves, but Charlie was no charismatic leader and failed to convince us that Peterhead would be a golden opportunity for career advancement.

We were despatched on spurious scouting visits to Buchan in pursuit of procuring possible pipe-yards, meeting and greeting mostly disbelieving and disgruntled smallholders with offers of untold riches. Some chance, as the leading farmer and stock-trader, Ewan Booth, had preference on all the premium sites and had already sold them to incoming property speculators. That was a salutary lesson in real estate negotiations.

Sidlaw had taken us in a minibus from Aberdeen to Dundee to join in the fun of an evening at their headquarters and to meet with their other junior management and share the joy of the announcement of the Group's annual financial statements. What larks!

# 14. Moving on up

Looking outwards at the many new organisations arriving in Aberdeen, I could see other young guys with lesser qualifications, experience and perceived potential, picking up prestigious positions with fancy salaries and benefits. The heady brew of envy, ambition, inertia and frustration boiled up to my consideration of abandoning the Asco pipe dream and looking for an alternative avenue of opportunity. There was no shortage of openings but the "gentleman's agreement" between Jim Simpson and his main clients meant that none of those would make any outright offer even though many were desperate for recruits. I started to apply for advertised positions and that led to a few interviews but nothing clicked.

I had by now formed an idea of my ideal job and that was to be a Materials Supervisor with an Operator. The oil companies (Operators) had the best conditions and benefits, but not always the best salaries, and offered the best prospects for career enhancement. The bigger the Operator, the safer the job, the surer the prospect of training and development; but there was a downside, as I had witnessed at Shell, in growing into a "Company Man," and no self-respecting hippy, even a cynical recalcitrant such as myself, would contemplate such a fate.

The next best option was with the Contractors, either drilling, diving or construction. Their pay rates were higher and the chances of early promotion higher but they were notoriously more capricious and demanding and they offered less job security. I figured I was still young enough to take a risk.

During September 1973 I recall receiving three direct job offers, all of which had higher wage rates and improved benefits and conditions over my position at Asco. Out of my respect for Jim Simpson, who had given me a job when there were no others, had put up with my mumps and moans, kept me employed when others might have told me to go away in short, jerky movements and had indulged my fanciful ideas for the development of his own corporate creation, I went to him and explained that I had reached the end of the road with Asco and had been offered chances to move on. I told him I would appreciate his advice as to which I should choose as my next employer. His response was typically succinct and apposite.

"John, don't worry about letting Asco down, I'm not even sure if I will still be here a year from now. Jimmy Gallan says you've done a fine job and that's fine by Maggie and me. You'll get a better job for sure but, before you decide where to go, have a word with Sedco."

"What about your gentlemen's agreement?"

"Oh, yes, well that was all well and good while there were only a few of us around, but things are all very different now. It's open warfare on the market and it's hard to get good folks. Sedco know what you can do and they're good people to work for. Go and have a word with Frank James and tell him I sent you."

With Jim's endorsement I stepped out into the lane and sought out Frank James. As I had not yet had much of a chance to get to know him I was going in with only a third party view of the man and, in the short time he had been in Aberdeen, he had earned a reputation to match his villainous name. He even looked like a gangster in the mould of Edward G Robinson playing Al Capone. I was only a little nervous as I already had three job offers to fall back on, but became a little more so as I sat down in Frank's office. He was not as overtly hospitable as Elmer or Virgil and the Pinteresque pauses that defined his speech pattern would make any interviewee edgy.

Within a few more minutes I began to relax and Frank set me at ease by saying that he had heard good reports from Elmer and Virgil that I could fit the bill for a particular job in the new Sedco regime. He outlined the plans for the new office being built at West Tullos and the refurbishment of the old Ladybird Factory in

Craigshaw Road that was now the new warehouse.

Without disclosing any trade secrets, as a lot of the new contracts were in final stages of negotiation, he indicated that Sedco would be increasing the size of their fleet and that as many as nine or ten of their giant rigs might end up in the North Sea. I had seen their existing rig, the venerable *135F*, and that was a monster; my mind boggled at the concept of being part of running a multi-rig operation. With the comfort of knowing that I would be working for people with whom I had gained mutual respect and with a contractor that had the world's top oil companies queuing up to hire their equipment I dropped the idea of taking up any of the other job offers.

We never really negotiated on salary and conditions. There would be no company car but, when Frank offered a rate of £50 per week plus overtime I just about snapped his hand off in instant agreement. He would fix it with Jim Simpson to waive my one-month notice period and I was cleared to move on within barely a week.

Things moved so fast I never had much of a chance for saying farewell but I do recall as I walked back down the lane retracing the path trodden nearly five years ago, weaving through executive cars where the wrecked lorries had lain and rotted, comparing the plush offices with the abandoned grain mill covered in pigeon-shit and thinking that some sort of miracle had occurred.

There were corners of Regent Road that still held obsolete equipment, abandoned in the face of industrial progress, but it was not the grain sifters (all sold to fund the Barytes Cutters Ball.) It was the elevators, augers and bulkers, brought in to cope with the surge in demand for drilling mud that caught my eye. All of that had been made redundant within only a few years, by the introduction of CEBO's automated bulk handling equipment. This was a fast moving business

I felt proud of what we had achieved over the past few years. I knew we had worked hard and was gratified in later years when some well informed contacts in this mighty industry explained that

Asco's efforts (Jimmy Gallan, in particular) in churning out great volumes of barytes during 1969 had helped ensure that Amoco could complete the difficult well that proved to be the "Montrose" discovery. They also told me that the 150 tons of brine that we managed to despatch on Hogmanay 1970 was critical in the completion of the "Argyll" discovery. The UK's first oilwells might have gone undiscovered without our efforts.

"Dubs" was now the past. Drilling was to be my future.

# INDEX

*I*

*II*

*III*

*IV*

*V*

*VI*

# Glossary

**Ain:** Own
**Aul:** Old

**Barytes:** Barium Sulphate
**Big, Biggin:** Build, building
**Birl:** Turn
**Blad:** Vandalise
**Bothy:** Workman's shack
**Burachie:** Gathering

**Cassies:** Cobbles
**Caul:** Cold
**Claes:** Clothes
**Connach:** Spoil
**Coont:** Count

**Dae:** Do
**Dat:** That
**Dinna, Dinnae:** Don't
**Dis:** This
**Doon:** Down
**Du:** You
**Dubs:** Mud

**Fan:** When
**Far, Faur:** Where
**Fit:** What
**Fitba:** Football
**Fit wye?:** Why
**Foo:** How
**Fower:** Four
**Fu, Fou:** Full

**Gaun:** Go, going
**Gey:** Awful, extreme

**Haud:** Hold
**Heid:** Head
**Hemmin:** Hey, you.

**Humph:** Lift
**Hunner:** Hundred

**Ken:** Know

**Loon:** Lad

**Mony:** Many
**Moonpool:** Lower deck opening
**Morn, the:** Tomorrow

**Nae:** No, not

**Ony:** Any
**Oorly:** Hourly

**Piece:** Sandwich
**Plitery:** Slithery

**Quine:** Girl

**Richt guid red oot:** Spring clean
**Rowie:** Morning roll
**Rug:** Tug
**Rucks:** Piles, stacks

**Scumphishing:** Sweltering
**Seck:** Sack
**Sharny:** Defecatory
**Shottie:** Try, turn
**Smoko:** Rest break

**Teuchter:** Country dweller
**Tint:** Lost
**Toon:** Town
**Toonser:** Town Dweller
**Twa:** Two

**Wadder:** Water